Collected Works Volume Five Further Studies

Nigel Pearce

chipmunkapublishing
the mental health publisher

Author Name

All rights reserved, no part of this publication may be reproduced by any means, electronic, mechanical photocopying, documentary, film or in any other format without prior written permission of the publisher.

>   Published by
>   Chipmunkapublishing
>   United Kingdom

http://www.chipmunkapublishing.com

Copyright © Nigel Pearce 2023

The debate between Antigone and Creon does not end with her death.

This thesis will endeavour to show the debates between Antigone and Creon continued across texts and modes of production. They indeed must until the material conditions which gave rise to them are resolved, as Louis MacNeice suggested in the second dawn of civilisation:

   Communism in its truest sense, is an effort to think, and to think into action human society as an organism[1].

Hegel described *Antigone* from a bourgeois dialectical position as 'celestial Antigone[2]' representing the ruling class family, Creon as the antithesis, *polis* and a higher synthesis of family and *polis*. Marx turned Hegel's dialectic on its head, thus placing Hegel's aesthetics and dialectic in material reality. This is the methodology employed in my thesis. It is derived from Marx, illustrated below in Jameson[3]

Superstructures	CULTURE IDEOLOGY (philosophy, religion, etc.) THE LEGAL SYSTEM POLITICAL SUPERSTRUCTURES AND THE STATE	
Base or infrastructure	THE ECONOMIC, OR MODE OF PRODUCTION	RELATIONS OF PRODUCTION (classes) FORCES OF PRODUCTION (technology, ecology, population)

contradiction which produces its own onward movement?

Poetry is clotted social history, the emotional sweat of man's struggle with Nature.' [5] Thus, for this thesis, each manifestation of Antigone is based on 'clotted' or concrete moments which are dialectically posed.

Nevertheless, Hellenistic Greece was a unique society. A direct democracy where the sacred was interwoven into everyday life. The Aristotelian structure of Greek tragedy as codified in Aristotle, *Poetics* [Fig 2 Freytag's Triangle] was integrated into this religious life:

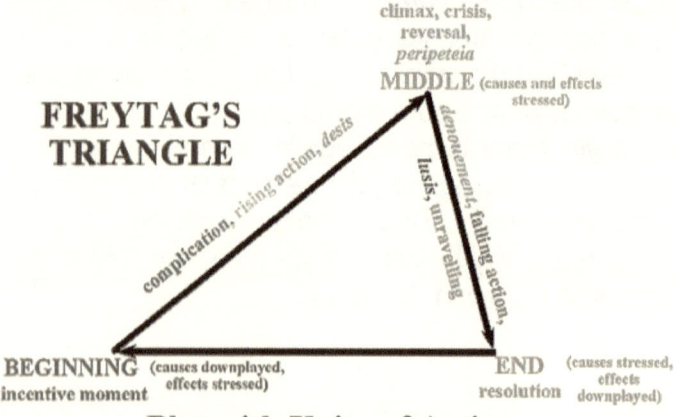

Plot with Unity of Action

[6]

It is of significance that Aristotle thought *Oedipus Rex*, also written by Sophocles to be the perfect play because Aristotle argued it illustrated three essential elements 1) unity of action 2) unity of time: the action in a play should take place in the span of a day and a night (this is important because the Athenian theatre was open air and consequently, 3) unity of place. Inherent in Hellenistic poetics was the predetermination of the major characters who were 'heroes' from a 'cultural store' of myths which were reinterpreted by different authors. Hence, we can see how Sophocles used irony. In *Antigone,* the audience sees the denouement on stage, yet the philosophical or ideological questions remain. Also, Sophocles introduced 'the third person' on stage, so Antigone is in dialogue with Ismene at the beginning, adding an extra dimension to the performance. Sophocles' play won the competition at the festival of Dionysus in 441 B.C., and as a result, he achieved fame as both a writer and a statesman. The first written records of the drama text of Antigone were not located until 1,500 years later. Problems of translation into English are evident by the period of time which elapsed before the first was taken from Latin by Thomas Watson in 1581.

Evidence of the dialectical conflict between Creon and Antigone in dramaturgy, literature and philosophy can be located in Steiner *Antigone*[7]. It is important, though, to note that the play was more nuanced than Creon simply as the antithesis of a revolutionary Antigone. Creon is transformed by *peripeteia* during the play, and Antigone takes her *physic* to its conclusion. Therefore, his defence of the *polis* changes over time in the context of a Hellenistic society which was a fusion of sacred and secular:

> The man who came to burn the pillars and treasures of their temples, to burn their country and scatter its laws to the winds? Can you see the gods honouring evil men?

> Impossible!
> Sophocles, L. 261-5.[8]

So Creon acted on religiopolitical grounds. Antigone was motivated substancially by religious purification and burial rites. The burial of Polyneices.

Steiner illustrated Antigone and Creon's dialectic in modernity by referencing Heinrich Boll's script which was used in the television series *Der Herbst in Deutschland* 1979[9] [The German Autumn] which explored the *Antigone* text and Marxism. I note that German audiences at that time would have been aware that the phrase 'German Autumn' referenced an attempt by the urban guerrilla group Red Army Faction/Socialist Patients Collective to topple the West German State. In this context, Ismene paradoxical imagery anticipated the play's conflicts.

> You have a *hot heart* for *chilling deeds*.[10]
> Sophocles.L88.

Jean Anouilh's play was written in 1942 during the Nazi occupation and to the dismay of the Communist Resistance, performed in Paris in 1944. Camus noted that in 1952 they were unhappy with its ramifications for the Vichy regime:

> Antigone is right – but Creon is not wrong.
> Anouilh *Antigone* p xiv[11]

In contrast to Sophocles, Anouilh employed the Prologue-Chorus, which was probably Anoulh's boldest innovation. As a single character who interacts with and comments on both the action and on the nature of drama, employing meta-theatre. Alternatively, Sophocles had begun with two sisters speaking outside the city, i.e. the 'public sphere'. Anoulth commences with a man commenting on all members of the cast. We later hear a cry of desperation from him:

> Don't let her die Creon! We will all bear the scar for thousands of years.
>
> Anouilh p.49

The chorus in Anouilh was aware of the conventions of tragedy and secularized the play. At the Premiere, in occupied Paris, he would know if Antigone was seen to die ignobly this would be a blow to the Resistance. However, Creon feared the 'mob' and despite the pleas from Haemon and the intervention of the Chorus he was ruthless in sacrificing Antigone to propitiate them. Here is an example of dramatic irony because intertextually the audience would have known the 'mob' were sympathetic to Antigone in Sophocles:

> Chorus. Can't you try to gain time, and have her escape, tomorrow.
>
> Creon. The mob knows already. They're all around the palace yelling. I can't turn back.
>
> Anouilh p.50.

What strikes is the use of the vernacular?

Creon might be a personification of the State or in Nazi occupation as Father/ Fuhrer:

> That **g**iant-**g**od.
>
> Anouilh, p.51.

Alliterative '**g**'s in the 'target' translation:
> Haemon (crying out like a child, throwing himself into Creon's arms)
> Oh, Father, it isn't true, it isn't you, it isn't happening.
> … I beg you to let me admire you still.
> Anouilh p. 52

The line commenced with an apostrophe 'Oh' continued with anapaestic feet asking three rhetorical questions demanding paternal reassurance:
> Creon (putting him away). You have looked up to your father too long. Look me straight in the eye. That is what it means to be a man.
> Anouilh p. 52.

This suggested a psychoanalytical moment which later manifested as an Oedipal Complex. Agreeing with Badiou that a Freudo-Marxist model with Creon perceived as a 'superego' had explanatory value:
> Here in the counterpart of the superego is the fact that the essence and the constitutive core of the State, the domination of one class by another is always dictatorial.[12]

Creon's 'look me straight in the eyes' resounded intertextually with Harrison[13] whose gaze of the 20th century's elites looked upon the world's innocents and petrified without pity. Harrison[14]:
> A verse commentary on the unspeakable horrors of the twentieth century:

> what are we doing with our art?
> are we still strumming the right lyre
> to play us through the century's fire?

The rhyme of lyre and fire stressed the contradictory relationship between art and war. Creon was implacable:

> Creon: She has spoken now. All Thebes knows what she's done...
>
> Creon: Your happiness as well as mine, you fool.
>
> Antigone: You disgust me, all of you, you and your happiness!'

Anouilh p.47.

Antigone and Haemon are the youth caught in familial conflicts and can be understood as trampling humanity. In Anouilh's Antigone, the dialogue between Creon and Antigone is longer than its Sophoclean 'source text'. This accommodated contemporary French Existentialism, which understood the world as absurd and the social agent is responsible for the consequences of their actions. Antigone embraced praxis. The 'love interest' between the couple and Creon's familial compassion represents a different tone to Sophocles. Haemon mirrored *Camera obscura* Antigone:

> Haemon - you can't let them take her away from me!

Here enjambment stresses the bourgeois individualism of 'me':

> Creon: Yes, my boy – I can. Come now – courage.

The caesuras emphasis Creon self-belief, almost arrogance:

Haemon: It is over already.
Anouilh, p. 51

The Prophet[15] illustrates an example of the prophet as an intertextual motif. A powerful figure in some epochs and an outcast in others. The ruling classes were often too blinded by their power and wealth to hear the prophet's words. So in Sophocles *Antigone* Creon had an almost paranoid belief that Teiresias was acting out of self-interest or money. The audience knew that Creon's integrity had been compromised because of Athenian perspectives about the afterlife. Having entombed Antigone who belongs in a world of mortals and prevented the journey, by the necessary burial rites, of her brother, Polyneices, to Hades. Still, Creon believed the prophet spoke falsely:

Creon: Be sure you will not buy off my resolve.

Tiresias: Know that you will not live through many more races of the sun before you give one born of your loins as a corpse of exchange for corpses!

Sophocles, L 1030-33.

This scanned because the origins of poetry were in the chants of Shaman:

Poetry has grown out of magic.[16]

Contrasting with the prosaic prose line spoken by Creon, whom the gods damned. He, too late, sought refuge in the 'established laws' (Sophocles, L 1074). He sought a "synthesis" that did not exist, one which would not generate further dialectical conflicts and that the condemnation of Teiresias made quite apparent:

> Such arrows have I fired like an archer at your heart, in anger, for you have provoked me; arrows which are true, and you shall not escape their sting.'
>
> Sophocles L. 1048-59

To remark on Antigone as a protagonist in Greek drama, where she would have been acted by a man in 5 B.C. with a mask, and whose 'voice' was silenced in that *performance text.* Sartre's position had cogency:

> that the ancient playwright had a relationship with his the audience, it was simply impossible to replicate.[17]

Yet as an intertextual voice because she found resonance in literary characters like Vera Pavlovna[18] or Nora[19]. They may not be 'sisters 'kin' but of 'struggle', forerunners of 'New Woman'. Dyadic opposites to Creon. I have attempted to show how my initial method was embellished by Freudo-Marxist and Feminist literary analysis and that the dialectic between Antigone and Creon continued in texts and was interpreted by other critics. Antigone can be 'read' as a secular revolutionary. One cannot forget she acted in 5. B.C. from conservative religious beliefs. The Cairo 2002[20] performance might have synthesised both political and religious aspects for the audience. MacNeice's second red dawn of civilisation remained a shimmer before tomorrow morning.

Bibliography.
Primary Texts.

Anouilh, J *Antigone* (trans Barbara Bray, London. Bloomsbury, 2013).

Aristotle, *Poetics* (trans Heath, M. London, Penguin Classics, 1996).

Sophocles, *Antigone*, (Cairo production, directed by Frank Bradley, 2002).

Sophocles, *Antigone* (trans, Brown, A.L Oxford, Oxbow Books, 2014).

Sophocles, *The Three Theban Plays: 'Antigone', 'Oedipus the King', 'Oedipus at Colonus'* (trans, Robert Fagles, London, Penguin Classics, 1984).

Sophocles, *Antigone* (trans David Franklin and John Harrison, Cambridge, Cambridge University Press, 2003).

Secondary Texts.

Badiou, A, *A Theory of the Subject* (London, Continuum, 2009).

Bernstein, J. M. *Hegel's Feminism* [Ed] Fanny Söderbäck Feminist Readings of Antigone (SUNY series in Gender Theory, State University of New York Press, 2010).

Blackledge, P, *Reflections on the Marxist theory of History* (Manchester, Manchester University Press, 2006).

Cairns, D, Sophocles: *Antigone* (Oxford, Bloomsbury, 2016).

Caudwell, C, *Illusion and Reality* (London, Lawrence & Wishart, 1946).

Chernyshevsky, N, *What Is to Be Done?* (Ithaca & London, Connell University Press.1989).

Clayton, J and Rothstein, E, 'Figures in the Corpus: Theories of Influence and Intertextuality', in *Influence and Intertextuality in Literary History* (Madison, WI: The University of Wisconsin Press, 1991).

de Sousa Correa and Owens, W.R. *The Handbook of Literary Research*, (London, Routledge and The Open University, 2010).

Deutscher, I. *The Prophet: The Life of Leon Trotsky* (London, Verso Books, 2015).

Garvie, A, F. *The Plays of Sophocles* (London, Bloomsbury, 2016).

Jameson, F. *The Political Unconscious: Narrative as a socially symbolic act* (London, Routledge Classics, 2002).

Hardwick, L and Fraser, R. Readings *for Block 1* (Milton Keynes, The Open University, 2010).

Hardwick, L and Fraser R. *Reading Guide for Block 1: Antigone across* worlds (Milton Keynes, The Open University, 2010).

Harrison, T. *The Gaze of the Gorgon*. (Newcastle-upon-Tyne: Bloodaxe Books, 1992).

Ibsen, H. *Four Major Plays: Doll's House; Ghosts; Hedda Gabler; and The Master Builder*, (Oxford, Oxford World's Classic, 2008).

MacNeice, L, *Selected Literary Criticism* Ed. Alan Heuser (Oxford, Clarendon 1987).

Steiner, G, *The Antigone Myth in Western Literature, Art and, Thought* (Oxford, Oxford University Press, 2003).

Swift, L *Greek Tragedy; Themes and Contexts,* (London, Bloomsbury, 2016).

Thompson, G, *Marxism and Poetry* (London. Lawrence & Wishart, 1946).

Williams, R, *Marxism and Literature* (Oxford: Oxford University Press, 1994).
Žižek, S, *Antigone* (London: Bloomsbury, 2016).

Hugh MacDiarmid the poetics of engagement and its methods:

On being 'myriad minded' in *Three Hymns to Lenin.*

Every door in any town should be wide open to that great lyric poet Hugh MacDiarmid, a light burning in every window, food and drink on each table, and a bed aired, with sheets. If only one could think of all the statues that will one day be put up to him all over Scotland, work out roughly how much these statues will cost and give him the money now. Posterity can look after itself: that is its function. Honour the brief lives now.

Dylan Thomas Hugh MacDiarmid: Second Hymn to Lenin (Spring 1960) (marxists.org)

One major shortcoming in my writing that focusing on *Three Hymns to Lenin. (1957)* may help to correct in my authorial practice is to 'focus' more and not 'be wildly subjective' as Chris pointed out in my last script. Writing with 'focus' is not always easy when writing through the prism of MH issues. However, hopefully, my study of this collection may help correct this problem. Although MacDiarmid had a breakdown in 1935, he wrote Second Hymn to Lenin. MacDiarmid in *Three Hymns to Lenin* (1957) deals with complex and convoluted material but stays eminently 'focused.' This is one of the many lessons I hope to learn from Hugh MacDiarmid.

Hugh MacDiarmid worked in a factory supporting the struggle against fascism during WW11. But as Chris has said his work was indeed wonderfully ambitious. He challenged the English Ascendancy in culture by writing in dialect and created the Scottish Renaissance. Two of his three hymns to Lenin were written in such dense dialect that I must use a Scots/English Dictionary to get a good close reading. It is well worth it though as this was not Socialist Realism as turned out by numerous other writers. The poem Chris mentioned 'A Drunk Man Looks at the Thistle' is renowned for its synthesis of Scots dialects with some English language. A giant of a poet by any estimation and considered to rank with Robert Burns in Scotland. But who am to speak from South of the border?

He has been reading to sharpen the clarity of his methodology for:

Master of Arts in Creative Writing.

Critical Reading Reflection.

'Hugh MacDiarmid the poetics of engagement and its methods:

On being 'myriad minded' in Three Hymns to Lenin.'

MacDiarmid makes an oblique but unfortunate reference to Trotsky in Three Hymns to Lenin (1957). However, MacDiarmid was a complex poet, and many of his comrades in the CPGB apparently said, 'they did not know what to make of him?' He was expelled twice. He had been influenced by the ideas of John Maclean. Still, with MacLean's death and the receding tide of class struggle in Scotland [both believed Scottish

Socialism would predate any British workers state], his ideas were less anchored. Although I agree with most critics, he was the most important Scot's poet since Robert Burns but was not in Brecht's category as a Leftist poet.

Hugh MacDiarmid: 'Three Hymns to Lenin', written throughout several years, but was first published in 1957 as a collection. They were certainly not facile Socialist Realism but profoundly complex works illustrating dialectic contradictions and, attempted synthesise of the poet, of aesthetics and of the Revolution. MacDiarmid was aware though of the paradox of the complexity of Modernist poetry and the language of the masses and he addresses this consistently. Bizarrely, I think, First Hymn to Lenin was first published in magazine form by the Rightist, if experimental poet and critic, T.S.Eliot. The publication date of this collection was not an accident. He joined, for the third time, the CPGB in 1956 and wrongly understood Hungarian workers revolution from below as a counter-revolution. Dismissing as 'sentimental' those who left the Party in protest.

'It only remains to perfect myself in this new mode. This is the poetry I want – all I can regard now as poetry at all, as poetry of to-day, not of the past, A Communist poetry that bases itself On the Resolution of the C.C. of the R.C.P. In Spring 1925: 'The Party must vigorously oppose toughness and contemptuous treatment Of the old cultural heritage as well as of the literary specialists. It must likewise combat the tendency Towards a purely hothouse proletarian literature.'

Hugh MacDiarmid (CP1, p. 615)

First hymn to Lenin fusion of Christ and Lenin and what will follow Communism., free men.

I'm afraid I must disagree with much of Nancy K. Gish's commentary on MacDiarmid's overtly political poems. However, drawing on primary sources she does make some noteworthy points on his early sense of alienation caused by his advanced reading age, 'lived in a different mental world altogether." [Lucky Poet, p.17].

'Close reading' of Hugh MacDiarmid, 'Second Hymn to Lenin' is complete. As I remember, not platitudinous as some Leftist poetry of the period was but here, MacDiarmid asks profound questions about the interaction of poets & poetry and the masses. His use of regular and italicised fonts is impressive.

<u>Second Hymn to Lenin (extract/beginning.)</u>

'Ah, Lenin, you were right. But I'm a poet,

(And you c'ud make allowances for that!)

[…]

Thou' yours comes first, I know it.

An unexamined life is no' worth ha 'in' [...]

(The unexamined life is not worth living is a dictum supposedly uttered by Socrates at his trial for impiety and corrupting youth, for which he was subsequently sentenced to death, as described in Plato's Apology (38a5–6).)

Are my poems spoken in the factories and fields,
               In the streets o' the toon?
Gin they're no', then I'm failin' to dae
               What I ocht to ha' dune.

[...]

'Haud on haud on; what poet's dune that?
               Is Shakespeare read,
Or Dante or Milton or Goethe or Burns?
               – You heard what I said.

[...]

Your knowledge in your ain sphere
Was exact and complete
But your sphere's elementary and sune by
As a poet man see't.

For a poet maun see in a'thing,
Ev'n what looks trumpery or horrid,
A subject equal to ony
– A star for the forehead!

A poet has nae choice left…

Final Stanza:

Unremittin', relentless,
Organized to the last degree.
Ah, Lenin, politics is bairns' play
To what this maun be!

<u>Second Hymn to Lenin (extract.)</u>

'You turned a whole world right side up, and did so

With no dramatic gesture, no memorable word.

Now measure Glasgow for a like laconic overthrow!

On days of revolutionary turning points you literally flourished,

Became clairvoyant, foresaw the movement of classes,

And the probable zig-zags of the revolution As if on your palm;

Not only an analytical mind but also

A great constructive, synthesizing mind Able to build up in thought the new reality As it must actually come

By force of definite laws eventually, […]'

Hugh MacDiarmid, (Lenin, II, 894).

    I like the way MacDiarmid used variants of Scottish dialects to undermine the colonial linguistic hegemony of Standard English. He wrote in Standard English on occasion.

Hugh MacDiarmid was a complex person. I have mentioned before that he liked the phrase 'myriad minded.' It is also clear that he was influenced by Rilke's maxim: 'the poet must know everything.' There was not the vast chasm some saw in his ideological proclivities when one understands that he believed in a 'synthesis', another favourite word, of Scottish Nationalism and a form of Marxism. In this, he was in the tradition of John Maclean and by once removed that of James Connolly.

Second Hymn to Lenin.

[...]

Trotsky – Christ, no' wi' a croon o' thorns
But a wreath o'paper roses.

An attack on Trotsky would be consistent with the Stalinist 'line' of the CPGB when it was written in 1932 to be published originally in 1935.

New Woman and Hobgoblins:

The Communist Manifesto in 19th-Century Britain and its literary aftermaths. A study of Helen Macfarlane and Eleanor Marx. (second verdion).

Abstract.

If women's liberation is unthinkable without Communism, then Communism is unthinkable without women's liberation.

- Inessa Armand quoted in Sharon Smith *Women and Socialism*

(Illinois, Haymarket Books (2015).

This thesis is of significance because it illuminates an important 'hidden history' of 19th-century 'New Woman' on the British Left employing the methodology of Marxism and its sister models as they developed across time until the late 20th century and into the 21st. It will explore recent studies of Helen Macfarlane and Eleanor Marx, their lives and writing and analyse them from a theoretical perspective rather than understanding them simply as historical figures. It will, therefore, attempt a dialectical synthesis of these elements. Thus, recognising the importance of the 'personal as political' but transcending that biographical category and understanding the fusion of Labour & literature. These two women will be shown, like Karl Marx and Frederick Engels, to have been polymaths and will attempt to delineate their demise employing the living tradition in which they had fought for socialism. This thesis will make a connection in terms of Althusserian problematics and concomitant symptomatic readings between the suicides of Eleanor Marx and Sylvia Plath. It will endeavour to further the knowledge of an internationalist and revolutionist tradition within Britain and ask why these two women leaders were almost lost to the modern scholar. I will employ the ideas of Marx, Engels, Luxemburg, Trotsky, Kollontai, Lukács, Althusser and Gramsci as the main structure for this analysis. However, I will also illustrate the impact of modern feminism from Simone de Beauvoir, Kate Millet, Elaine Schowalter, Lise Vogel and then 21st century Marxist feminists Sharon Smith and Judith Orr in reaching my conclusion. That in 'the last instant' women's oppression can only be resolved in a qualitatively different society. Thus, Lukács insight that this would be 'the-identical-subject-object of history', socialism. Helen Macfarlane and Eleanor Marx will be shown to be the equals of the intellectually advanced elements of the British, the international Left. I shall argue they were oppressed by patriarchy and capitalism.

Contents.

Introduction.

Soundings.

Thesis and methodology. Marx and Engels in Britain during the 1840s and Chartism. Communist Manifesto and its Histories. a) Relationship to The League of the Just. b) Engels' early drafts c) An evolution of Prefaces.

Chapter One.

Kant and Hegel in Britain.

Helen Macfarlane and her translations of Hegel, the Communist Manifesto and other writings including critiques of Carlyle and literary texts. Conclusion: Utopian-Socialism, not Scientific Socialism, somewhat akin to George Elliot's translation of Strauss and Feuerbach and that milieu. No evidence that the two met but were published in contending London papers *The Leader* & *Red Republican.* There is textual material to suggest that Elliot thought Macfarlane too radical. Interestingly they both returned to the dominant ideology of their epoch, Christianity either directly or more ambiguously.

Chapter Two.

Death and Resurrection in Nantwich.

Helen Macfarlane's Legacy. Personal tragedies then married a vicar, but the seeds were already there in her earlier written works. So consistent Utopian Socialist /Bourgeois Idealist.

Chapter Three.

Eleanor Marx: A Dreamer of Absolutes.

A 'new wave' of proletarian struggle: the Paris Commune 1870, she writes *Shelley's Socialism*. Bloody Sunday in London, 1880's. Eleanor Marx as the embodiment of Marxist 'praxis'. Conflict with Althusserian R.S.A.

Chapter Four

Ibsen's *Doll's House*. A Study in Patriarchy.

Eleanor Marx was the victim of being unconsciously *interpellated by Patriarchy* so although able to lead worker's' movements she was unable to defy Edward Aveling sexist behaviour and when the class struggle waned her only consolation was the grave. The Althusserian problematic of the epoch would not be answered by the Paris Commune. The silences could only be answered with the symptomatic reading of the narrative that began in 1917. Too late for Eleanor Marx. Eleanor Marx and Aveling claimed to be Ibsenites. At the first English reading of A *Doll's* House given in their Chancery Lane lodgings in 1886. Eleanor read Nora, Aveling (portentously) Helmer and Bernard Shaw, Krogstad.

Notes on Method.

One key concept is '*the problematic*' that Althusser described thus: 'the objective internal reference system of its particular themes, the system of questions commanding the answers given.' (Althusser, *For Marx, 1979, p.67n).* By this, he meant an objective structure which allows what can be 'said' or not. As Callinicos describes:

> The problematic of a theory is objective: it cannot be reduced to the beliefs of the author of the theory; it is extractable only by means of a symptomatic reading.'[1]

So, as Luke Ferretter (2006, p.35-36) points out some of Sylvia Plath's more violent imagery before her suicide in 1963 could be explained through a symptomatic reading in that she did not have a second wave feminist 'problematic' to answer her writing, it did not exist. As Althusser maintained:

---

[1] Alex Callinicos, *Althusser's Marxism (*1976). p, 35.

> Every ideology must be regarded as a real whole, internally unified by its own problematic, so that it is impossible to extract one element without altering its meaning.[2]

I shall suggest Eleanor Marx's suicide was similar to Sylvia Plath's because she did not have a revolutionary 'problematic' or an alternative system to answer her questions. Thus, a 'symptomatic' reading illustrates the Paris Commune had failed and a new problematic was not formed until October 1917. Hence, in Althusserian terms:

> (A symptomatic reading) divulges the undivulged event in the text it reads, and in the same movement relates it to a *different text*, present as a necessary absence of the first.[3]

Chapter Five.

Hot Autumn: Alexandra Kollontai, the Doll's House Unlocked.

Kollontai in the context of the early Russian revolution provided the key to unlock the Doll's House. The Stalinist counter-revolution locked it again.

---

[2] Althusser, Louis *For Marx,* p, 62.
[3] Althusser and Balibar *Reading Capital* (2009) p.52.

Conjectures and Reawakening:

Simone de Beauvoir, *The Second Sex.*

Kate Millet, *Sexual Politics,*

Elaine Showalter, *A Literature of Their Own.*

Lise Vogel, *Marxism, and the Oppression of Women: Towards a Unitary Theory.*

Sharon Smith, *Women and Socialism.*

Judith Orr, *Marxism and Women's Liberation.*

Conclusion:

Both Helen Macfarlane and Eleanor Marx were committed, revolutionary socialists. In leadership roles. However, in terms of their belief systems, they failed. Helen 'sold out.' Eleanor committed suicide. In *The Myth of Sisyphus* Albert Camus argued: 'The consequences of realization are suicide or recovery.' For these two revolutionaries to have stood on the peaks of class struggle and seen it evaporate would have been overwhelming. Helen Macfarlane sought solace in illusion, her alienated species - being (Feuerbach/Marx/Freud) religion buried at St. Michael's Church, Baddeley, just outside Nantwich. 'Tussey', ever the active agent, (her motto: 'Always ahead') took her own life, I suggest because, in the 'last instant' her life was revolution and literature and thus because of the downturn in class-struggle and the rise of Aestheticism there was no hope. These women, although significant figures on the Left, were doubly oppressed, by Capital and Patriarchy. I thus, find a degree of explanatory value in 'dual systems theory' school of socialist – feminism. However, a solution can only be found when the proletariat acts as a 'class-for-itself' and becomes what Lukács, called, the 'identical-subject-object of history.' As Trotsky noted this is neither a mechanistic nor voluntarist process:

The progress of a class toward class consciousness, that is, the building of a revolutionary party which leads the proletariat is a complex and a contradictory process. The class itself is not homogeneous. Its different sections arrive at class consciousness by different paths and at different times.[4]

Afterword

Hence, I have attempted to create a dialectical synthesis of theory and 'lived experience.' A literary praxis in this thesis which illustrates both 'hidden histories' of women in the British Left during the 19th century and provides the theoretical apparatus with which to do so. I have, also, drawn parallels with Patriarchal oppression in Eleanor Marx and Sylvia Plath and their deaths. However, conclusively, I locate the

---

[4] Trotsky, Leon, *What Next* (1932)
https://www.marxists.org/archive/trotsky/germany/1932-ger/index.htm

demise of both Helen Macfarlane and Eleanor Marx in the failure of the Marxist current within the British proletariat to generalise into the wider working-class movement and thus create the potential for the emancipation of all the oppressed. Because, as Eleanor Marx argued when the engines of proletarian gender and class interests are united:

> We are not women arrayed in struggle against men but we are in struggle against the exploiters.[5]

Thus, when the proletariat is united as a 'class-for itself', it would discover its inherent or 'ascribed consciousness' and lead the festival of the oppressed in creating 'the-identical-subject-object' of history' (Lukács), socialism. A dialectical synthesis has been attempted between 'the lived experience' of these women and the 'metanarratives' of Marxism and Feminism. These models have been shown to provide an analytical counterpoint to the dissonance of oppression, estrangement, and exploitation. We may recollect Walter Benjamin: 'There is no document of civilisation which is not at the same time a document of barbarism…A historical materialist regards it as his task to brush history against the grain.' [6]. This remains

---

[5] Eleanor Marx: How Should We Organize?" in Hal Draper, Women and Class, p309.
[6] Theses on the Philosophy of History VII in (ed) Arendt Walter Benjamin *illuminations*, (1999). p.248

Bibliography
Primary Sources

Adoratsky. V, *The History of the Communist Manifesto of Marx, and Engels*, (New York, International Publishers, 1938).

Bebel, August *Women and Socialism* (New York, Socialist Literature Company.1910).

Black, David [ed] *Helen Macfarlane Red Republican* (London, Unkant Publishers, 2014).

Chernyshevsky, Nikolay, *What is to Be Done, 1888.*
https://archive.org/details/cu31924096961036

Engels, Frederick *Socialism: Utopian and Scientific*

https://www.marxists.org/archive/marx/works/1880/soc-utop/index.htm

Engels, F, *The Origins of the Family, Private Property and The State* (Moscow, Progress Publishers, 1968).

Feuerbach, Ludwig *The Essence of Christianity* (trans) Elliot, George (Dover Philosophical Classics 2008).

Flaubert, Gustave *Madame Bovary* [Eleanor Marx-Aveling translation] Second Norton Critical Edition

[ed] Cohen, M, (New York, W.W. Norton & Company, 2005).

Democratic Review 1849-1850 [ed] Julian Harney, (New York, Barnes and Noble, 1968).

Harney Papers [ed] Black, F & Black, R (Assen, Royal Vangorcum Ltd, 1969).

Red Republican and The Friend of the People Vols 1 & 2 1850-1851 [ed] Julian Harney. Reprint with an introduction by John Saville (London, Merlin Press, 1966).

Ibsen, Henrik *A Doll's House, and Other Plays* (London, Penguin Classics, 2016).

Hegel, G.W.F. Phenomenology *of the Spirit* (Cambridge. Cambridge University Press, 1994).

Hobsbawm, Eric [ed] *The Communist Manifesto* (London, Verso, 2012).

Macfarlane, Helen Remarks on the times – Apropos of Certain Passages in No.1 of Thomas Carlyle's Latter-day Pamphlets *Democratic Review, June 1850*. [Black [ed] 2014).

Macfarlane, Helen, 'Chartism in 1850', *Red Republican*, 22nd June 1850.

Howard Morton" (Helen Macfarlane), "Fine Words (Household of otherwise) Butter No Parsnips." *Red Republican*, 20 July 1850.

Macfarlane, Helen The Communist Manifesto, *Red Republican*, [November 1850, 9th, 16th, 23rd & 30th] (London, Merlin Press, 1966).

MacLellan, David [ed]*The Communist Manifesto* (Oxford, Oxford World Classics, 2014).

The Daughters of Marx Selected Correspondence (ed) Olga Merrier & Faith Evans (Harmondsworth, Penguin *Books*, 1984).

Eleanor Marx & Edward Aveling, *Letters from England 1895* (London, Lawrence & Wishart, 2020).

Eleanor Marx & Edward Aveling *The Working-Class Movement in America* (London, Swan Sonenshein & Co, 1891).

Eleanor Marx & Edward Aveling *The Women Question from a Socialist Point of View*, 1886.

https://www.marxists.org › archive › eleanor-marx › works › womanq

Marx, Karl *'The Afterword' of the Second Edition of Capital Vol I* (Harmondsworth, Penguin Books, 1976).

Marx & Engels *Collected Works in 50 volumes*. (London, Lawrence & Wishart, 2004).

Marx & Engels *On Literature and Art. A Selection of Writings*, [eds] L. Baxandall and S. Mora (St. Louis, Milwaukee, 1973)

Marx & Engels, *Selected Correspondence* (Moscow, Progress Publishers, 1965).

Moore, Samuel in cooperation with Engels *The Communist Manifesto* (London, 30th January 1888).
https://www.marxists.org/archive/marx/works/1848/communist-manifesto/

Ryazanoff, D *Karl Marx: Man, Thinker and Revolutionist, a Symposium.* (London, Martin Lawrence Limited, 1927).

The Commonweal 1887 (The Official Journal of the Socialist League), (India, Pranava Books Classic Reprints, 2019).

The Commonweal (Journal of the Socialist League).

https://www.marxists.org/history/international/social-democracy/commonweal.htm

Socialist League (UK) Archives.
http://hdl.handle.net/10622/ARCH01344

The Socialist League Address to the Trade Unions (London. Socialist League Office, 1885, *Socialist Platform Reprints No. 1,* 1977).

The Socialist League Leaflets and Manifestos: An Annotated Checklist (Author) Eugene D. Lemire *International Review of Social History, Vol. 22, No 1 (1977).*

Secondary Sources.

Alexander, Sally (2007) Eleanor Marx's Political Legacy self-sacrifice or self-realisation. *Women's History Review.*

Althusser, Louis, *For Marx* (London, Verso, 1979).

Althusser, Louis, *Ideology and Ideological State Apparatuses (Notes Towards an Investigation [1970)*

Althusser, Louis, *Lenin and Philosophy and other essays* (Delhi, Askari Books 2009).

Althusser and Balibar *Reading Capital* (London, Verso, 2009).

Beauvoir, Simone de *The Second Sex. (London, Vintage Classics, 1997).*

Benjamin, Walter, *Illuminations*, [ed] Arendt Hannah (London, Pimlico, 1999).

Black, David *Helen Macfarlane A Feminist, Revolutionary Journalist, and Philosopher in Mid-Nineteenth Century England* (Oxford, Lexington Books, 2004).

Black, David, Ben Watson [*Radical Philosophy 187, (Sept/Oct 2014)* Helen Macfarlane

https://www.radicalphilosophy.com › article › helen-macfarlan

Brown, Heather A., *Marx on Gender, and the Family; A Critical Study* (Chicago, Haymarket Books, 2013).

Brown, Siobhan *A Rebel's Guide to Eleanor Marx* (London, Bookmarks, 2015).

Callinicos, Alex, *Althusser's Marxism,* (London, Pluto Press, 1976).

Callinicos, Alex *Social Theory: A Historical Introduction.* (Cambridge, Polity Press, 2012).

Camus, Albert, *The Myth of Sisyphus* (London, Penguin Great Ideas, 2005).

Carver, Terrell, & Farr, James *The Cambridge Companion to The Communist Manifesto.* (Cambridge, Cambridge University Press, 2015).

Cowling, Mark *The Communist Manifesto New Interpretations* (Cambridge, Edinburgh University Press, 1998).

Draper, Hal, *The Adventures of the Communist Manifesto* (California Centre for Socialist History, 2004).

Ferretter, Luke *Louis Althusser* (London, Routledge, 2006).

Foley, Barbara, *Marxist Literary Criticism Today* (London, Pluto Press, 2019).

Foot, Paul *The Vote* (London, Bookmarks, 2006).

Ginsburgh, Nicola, (2014) http://isj.org.uk/lise-vogel-and-the-politics-of-womens-liberation

Holmes, Rachel *Eleanor Marx A Life*, (London, Bloomsbury, 2014.)

Kapp, Yvonne *Eleanor Marx, A Biography*, (London, Verso, 2018.).

Selected Writings of Alexandra Kollontai
(Westport, Holt, Alix [ed] CT: Lawrence Hill & Co., 1977).

Alexandra Kollontai on Women's Liberation [ed] Rosenberg, Chanie (London, Bookmarks, 1977).

V I Lenin, *The Emancipation of Women* (International Publishers, 1984).

Lukács, Georg *History and Class Consciousness* (Pontypool, The Merlin Press, 2010).

Lukács, Georg *The Meaning of Contemporary Realism,* (Pontypool, The Merlin Press, 2006).

McLellan, David *Marx before Marxism* (Harmondsworth, Penguin Books, 1970).

Millett, Kate *Sexual Politics, (Urbana and Chicago, University of Illinois Press,* 2000).

Orr, Judith *Marxism and Women's Liberation.* (London, Bookmarks, 2015).

Prawer, S.S. *Karl Marx and World Literature.* (London, Verso, 2015).

Schoyen, A.R. *The Chartist Challenge,* (London, Heinemann, 1958).

Showalter, Elaine *A Literature Of Their Own: British Women Novelists from Brontë to Lessing.* (London, Virago, Revised Edition 2009).

Smith, Sharon *Women and Socialism* (Illinois, Haymarket Books, 2015).

Sullivan, Terry & Gluckstein, Donny *Hegel and Revolution* (London, Bookmarks, 2020).

Thatcher, Ian D. "Uneven and combined development", *Revolutionary Russia*, Vol. 4 No. 2, 1991.

Thompson E.P. (1976).

https://www.marxists.org › archive › thompson-ep › eleanor-marx "

Trotsky, Leon *Class and Art* (Speech, May 9th, 1926).

Trotsky, Leon, *Leon Trotsky on China*, (New York Pathfinder,1976).

Trotsky, Leon *Results and Prospects* http://www.marxists.org/archive/trotsky/1931/tpr/rp-index.htm

Trotsky, Leon, *What Next (*1932) https://www.marxists.org/archive/trotsky/germany/1932-ger/index.htm

Tsuzuki, Chuschichi *The Life of Eleanor Marx: A Socialist Tragedy*, (Oxford, Clarendon Press, 1967).

Vogel, Lise, *Marxism, and the Oppression of Women: Towards a Unitary Theory*. (Illinois, Haymarket Books, 2013).

Williams, Raymond *Problems of Materialism* (London, Verso 1980).

Hugh MacDiarmid the poetics of engagement and its methods:

On being 'myriad minded' in *Three Hymns to Lenin. (2)*

Hugh MacDiarmid used the phrase 'myriad minded' frequently which was reminiscent of Brecht ' A man with one theory is lost. He must have several, four, many.'

Hugh MacDiarmid used to like quoting Thomas Hardy, namely that literature was:

'the written expression of revolt against accepted things.'

Fools regret my poetic change – from my "enchanting early lyrics" / But I have found in Marxism all that I need'

- Hugh MacDiarmid.

Hugh MacDiarmid: 'Three Hymns to Lenin', written throughout a number of years, but was first published in 1957 as a collection. They were certainly not facile Socialist Realism but profoundly complex works illustrating dialectic contradictions and, attempted synthesise of the poet, of aesthetics and of the Revolution. MacDiarmid was aware though of the paradox of the complexity of Modernist poetry and the language of the masses and he addresses this consistently. Bizarrely, I think, First Hymn to Lenin was first published in magazine form by the Rightist, if experimental poet and critic, T.S.Eliot. The publication date of this collection was not an accident. He joined,for the third time, the CPGB in 1956 and wrongly understood Hungarian workers revolution from below as a counter-revolution. Dismissing as 'sentimental' those who left the Party in protest. One of which was my Uncle Reg on my mother's side who by the time I met him still knew his dialectics as taught by Maurice Cornforth but had degenerated and become a businessman. However, do not think it is just Tankies who swerve off course into the swamp.

It only remains to perfect myself in this new mode. This is the poetry I want – all I can regard now as poetry at all, As poetry of to-day, not of the past, A Communist poetry that bases itself On the Resolution of the C.C. of the R.C.P. In Spring 1925: 'The Party must vigorously oppose toughness and contemptuous treatment Of the old cultural heritage as well as of the literary specialists. . . It must likewise combat the tendency Towards a purely hothouse proletarian literature.'

Hugh MacDiarmid (CP1, p. 615)

First hymn to Lenin fusion of Christ and Lenin and what will follow Communism. Anarchism, free men.

'close reading' of Hugh MacDiarmid, 'Second Hymn to Lenin ' is complete. As I remember, not platitudinous as some Leftist poetry of the period was here, MacDiarmid asks profound questions about the interaction of poets & poetry and the masses. His use of regular and italicised fonts is impressive.

I'm afraid I have to disagree with much of Nancy K. Gish's commentary on MacDiarmid's overtly political poems. However, drawing on primary sources she does make some noteworthy points on his early sense of alienation caused by his advanced reading age, 'lived in a different mental world altogether." [Lucky Poet, p.17].

It only remains to perfect myself in this new mode. This is the poetry I want – all I can regard now as poetry at all, As poetry of to-day, not of the past, A Communist poetry that bases itself On the Resolution of the C.C. of the R.C.P. In Spring 1925: 'The Party must vigorously oppose Thoughtless and contemptuous treatment Of the old cultural heritage As well as of the literary specialists. . .. It must likewise combat the tendency Towards a purely hothouse proletarian literature.'

Hugh MacDiarmid (CP1, p. 615).

Second Hymn to Lenin (extract/beginning.)

'Ah, Lenin, you were right. But I'm a poet,

(And you c'ud make allowances for that!)

[…]

Thou' yours comes first, I know it.

An unexamined life is no' worth ha 'in' [...]

(The unexamined life is not worth living is a dictum supposedly uttered by Socrates at his trial for impiety and corrupting youth, for which he was subsequently sentenced to death, as described in Plato's Apology (38a5–6).)

I like the way MacDiarmid used variants of Scottish dialects to undermine the colonial linguistic hegemony of Standard English. He wrote in Standard English on occasion.

'Myriad minded' was a favourite phrase of his. Hugh MacDiarmid was a complex person. I have mentioned before that he liked the phrase 'myraid minded.' It is also clear that he was influenced by Rilke's maxim: 'the poet must know everything.' There was not the vast chasm some saw in his ideological proclivities when one understands that he believed in a synthesis, another favourite word, of Scottish Nationalism and a form of Marxism. In this, he was in the tradition of John Maclean and by once removed James Connolly.

'You turned a whole world right side up, and did so
With no dramatic gesture, no memorable word.

Now measure Glasgow for a like laconic overthrow!

On days of revolutionary turning points you literally flourished,

Became clairvoyant, foresaw the movement of classes,

And the probable zig-zags of the revolution As if on your palm;

Not only an analytical mind but also

A great constructive, synthesizing mind Able to build up in thought the new reality As it must actually come

By force of definite laws eventually, […]'

Hugh MacDiarmid, (Lenin, II, 894).

On the nature of poetics.

There is no money in poetry, but there is no poetry in money either.

- Robert Graves.

I would suggest that Robert Graves made a pertinent comment but lacked the methodology for understanding the nature of aesthetics. Thus, an appraisal of the creative processes involved in my authorial development over the MA in Creative Writing involves something rather more complex. The obvious question is what is art and, more especially, poetry? How does this mould my, indeed, anyone's artistic production and how can this change over time? Once I have asked this question and answered it, I will be able to appraise my poetics in the light of the two major sources of my dissertation: William Wordsworth and William Carlos Williams and my poetics in these contexts. I will seek a methodology, principally but not exclusively, in the writings of Karl Marx, Frederick Engels, Leon Trotsky and György Lukács. I will argue that there is a gulf between how bourgeois and Marxist literary criticism understand poetics. However, this has its foundations in a profound difference in Weltanschauung or worldview and that this 'in the last instance' is determined by the socio-economic relations of an epoch. However, it cannot be reduced to them because Marxism and Marxist aesthetics are far more complex than any reductive model.

I will also understand William Wordsworth (1802) *Preface to Lyrical Ballads https://en.wikisource.org/wiki/Preface_to_The_Lyrical_Ballads*

in which he argued for employing 'the language of ordinary men' and in *The Prelude* (1805) made the introspective turn. Writing in the shadow of John Milton (1667 / 1674), *Paradise Lost created* the foundation for what was to follow in Anglophone verse. In a new poetic revolution Ezra Pound urged poets at the beginning of the next century 'to make it new.' and in Retrospect (1918) wrote:

"1) Direct treatment of the 'thing' whether subjective or objective 2) To use absolutely no word that did not contribute to the presentation 3) As regarding rhythm: to compose in sequence of the musical phrase, not in sequence of a metronome." Here is possibly the best-known poem in which Ezra Pound implemented his manifesto:

In a Station of the Metro

The apparition of these faces in the crowd:
Petals on a wet, black   bough.

— *Poetry* (April 1913)

I shall, also, use the poetry of James Wright as a sympathetic counterpoint to my own and as a means of illustrating both my authorial choices and maturation

> Marx did not leave a systematic aesthetic; however, Marx was deeply influenced by both poetry and literature[1]. In his youth and young adulthood, Marx wrote poetry[2]. His

enduring friendship with Heinrich Heine is illustrative of this characteristic of Karl Marx's thinking and personality. However, where do we begin without a systematic poetic? The response is straightforward and is derived from György Lukács' (1921) *History and Class Consciousness: Studies in Marxist Dialectics.*

Let us assume for the sake of argument that recent research had disproved once and for all every one of Marx's individual theses. Even if this were to be proved, every serious 'orthodox' Marxist would still be able to accept all such modern findings without reservation and hence dismiss all of Marx's theses in toto – without having to renounce his orthodoxy for a single moment. Orthodox Marxism, therefore, does not imply the uncritical acceptance of the results of Marx's investigations. It is not the 'belief' in this or that thesis, nor the exegesis of a 'sacred' book. On the contrary, orthodoxy refers exclusively to method.

-
https://www.marxists.org/archive/lukacs/works/history

Thus, there is a method in Marxist analysis and that is its fundamental nature. For György Lukács' that was Historical Materialism because he questioned Frederick Engels position on the scientific validity of Dialectical Materialism. This is a fascinating controversy within Marxism, but I do not have the space to articulate it with any justice. I will only say I accept much of György Lukács' work but also agree with the general direction of Engel's investigations and codifications of Dialectical Materialism (Marx did not use the phrase) and Engel's positions, particularly the later letters, will bolster my argument in illustrating a Marxian poetic. However, György Lukács' (1921) *History of Class Consciousness* and its emphasis 'on method' although vital does not nullify the reality Marx's and others actual texts are incredibly significant for the poet and critic. Here we see Marx writing lyrically about Milton, *Paradise Lost* in this quite late text of 1862 & 1863.

> Milton produced *Paradise Lost* in the way that a silkworm produces silk as the expression of his own nature.

- Marx, Karl, *Theories of Surplus Value,* Moscow, Progress Publishers, 1963, p. 401.

This does not seem to resonant, immediately, with either Historical or Dialectical Materialism but as Molyneux, John (2020) p 43. argued cogently:

Of course, this is a rather inaccurate way of describing the writing of poetry; however, he clearly means by this that it was labour in which Milton affirmed and expressed himself (i.e., unalienated labour), and he insists that the character of this labour is not changed by the subsequent fact that the product is sold as a commodity. The second distinction is between Milton (the artist) and the 'literary proletarian' who 'delivers hackwork' on the orders of a publisher. In practice these distinctions may not be simple or absolute, with intermediate cases where the pressures of the market react back on the writer or artist without totally controlling their work, as is the case with normal wage labour. Nevertheless, they point to features that are typical of the situation of the artist under capitalism.

Here we are perceiving an innovative Marxist aesthetic. I shall delineate the origins and conclusions of John Molyneux (2020), *Dialectics of Art*. His first steppingstone in developing a new Marxian poetic was to reference Trotsky's often neglected contributions to the field of aesthetics:

> 'Another important influence was Leon Trotsky. Trotsky's main influence on me was in terms of revolutionary theory, but his Literature and Revolution and his essays in Leon Trotsky on Literature and Art made a huge impression. I very much agreed with his vehement defence of artistic freedom…and his insistence that art should be judged according to the 'law of art'. However, I don't think Trotsky, who had rather a lot of other things on his plate, ever really explained what the 'law of art' was. Anyway, it got me

> thinking, and some of the results can be seen in this book. - Molyneux, John. (2020) The Dialectics of Art (p. 11). Haymarket Books. Kindle Edition.

For Molyneux (2020), the question is, refreshingly, is artistic labour under capitalism 'alienated labour power' or 'non-alienated labour power'. This has significant ramifications for my poetics and concomitant creative processes and authorial choices as I will elaborate upon later in this paper. For Molyneux artistic labour-power' is not estranged from the poet or artist in the same manner that the majority of proletarians are alienated from their 'labour power'. They are alienated from the product of their labour, from each other and Nature. The proletarian's experience of capitalism is far greater than economic exploitation as expressed in Marx's Labour Theory of Value. But here we have the foundation for the Marxian understanding of creativity. As Marx so well encapsulated it as early in his maturation as 1844:

> The entire so-called history of the world is nothing but the creation of man through human labour.

- Karl Marx, Economic and Philosophic Manuscripts of 1844 Moscow: Progress Publishers, 1967, p. 106.

Lord Byron's and John Clare's *Don Juan*: a question of class.

Why did John Clare suffer from the delusion that he was Lord Byron during the last twenty-seven years of his life? The majority of these were spent in High Beech Asylum and Northampton County Asylum. Lord Byron and John Clare, who both achieved similar 'print-run' statistics at their height. One would become the first literary media celebrity and in his own time created the phenomena Byronism. The other would descend into insanity. Byron's sales with the publisher John Murray in 1819 alone for *Don Juan* Cantos 1 and 2 were in total 5,100 (production figure). The first edition was an expensive 31.5 shillings [1,350 copies] and then a cheaper 9.5 shillings [3,750 copies][7]. This reinforced his position as the dominant poet of those years. He had after the success of *Childe Harold's Pilgrimage* in 1812 said: 'I awoke one morning and found myself famous.'[8] However, John Clare, a 'labourer poet' had production figures from 1820-1835 of a regular 3,000 per edition but falling away until a posthumous collected edition in 1873 with figures n/a[9]. Both wrote versions of *Don Juan*, Clare's was clearly the creation of an ill man.

---

[7] St. Clair, William *The Reading Nation in the Romantic Period*, (Cambridge, Cambridge University Press, 2007), p. 327

[8] MacCarthy, Fiona, *Byron Life and Legend*. (London, John Murray, 2004). Introduction, p, x.

[9] St. Clair (2007), p. 592-597

How are we to understand these paradoxes? The methodological foundation for my analysis is drawn from Karl Marx

> we proceed from the active man... Consciousness does not determine life: life determines consciousness.[10]

Thus, we understand a socio-economic basis for culture. I will illustrate that argument was developed through Antonio Gramsci and by Raymond Williams into Cultural Materialism. Specifically, here, Gramsci's concept of 'contradictory consciousness' i.e., when a worker or a 'labourer poet' like John Clare can sustain both progressive and reactionary beliefs simultaneously. Frederick Engels had maintained that "false consciousness' could keep the working class from recognizing and rejecting their oppression.'[11] Antonio Gramsci developed this idea further:

The active man-in-the-mass has a practical activity, but has no clear theoretical consciousness of his practical activity, one might almost say that he has two theoretical consciousnesses (or one contradictory consciousness): one which is implicit in his activity and which unites him with all his fellow workers in the practical transformation of the real

---

[10] Marx, Karl & Engels, F The *German Ideology* (London. Lawrence & Wishart,1982), p.47
[11] Heywood, Andrew, *Political Ideas and Concepts: An Introduction, (London*, Macmillan, 1994) p.174.

world; and one, superficially explicit or verbal, which he has inherited from the past and uncritically absorbed.[12]

Therefore, we will comprehend a 'labourer poet' once he had not only quite normal 'contradictory consciousness' but was also estranged from his class after futilely looking towards the intelligentsia of his day who did not accept him. Here a second paradox appears as noted by Merryn & Raymond Williams[13]. This was that John Clare was estranged from his 'class' but not accepted into literary society. Then these contradictions once internalized would cause havoc. They were contradictions that are quintessential to class societies, that is pre-communist ones:

The history of all hitherto existing society is the history of class struggles. Freeman and slave, patrician and plebeian, lord and serf, guild-master and journeyman, in a word, oppressor and oppressed, stood in constant opposition to one another, carried on an uninterrupted, now hidden, now open fight...[14]

---

[12] Gramsci, Antonio Selections from the Prison Notebooks

[13] Clare *John, Selected Poetry and Prose [ed]*, Williams Merryn & Raymond (London, Methuen, 1986) pp 10-20.

[14] Marx, Karl & Engels Frederick *The Communist Manifesto* (Harmondsworth, Penguin Books, 1967) p, 79.

Thus, we see these two poets originated from opposite poles of the class spectrum, Lord Byron educated at Harrow and Cambridge while John Clare came from the rural poor. However, both classes were experiencing the transforming consequences of the Industrial Revolution. While the aristocracy would eventually come to an accord with the bourgeoisie the rural poor as a class was decimated with many becoming proletarians by the end of John Clare's life. Raymond Williams argues in *The Country and The City* (Chapter 13, 2016) this had a profound effect on 'pastoral poetry' with John Clare marking the end of the English Pastoral. Ultimately, he could not, Raymond Williams suggested, survive: 'in the noise of the market, profit, malice, envy, of capitalism'[15]. Raymond Williams concluded persuasively:

He lost his sanity, and this became manifest through the prism of Byronism with Clare deluded he was Byron.

Following Plato 'In vain does one knock at the gates of poetry with a sane mind' [Plato, *Phaedrus*, 245a][16]. We are provided with a shaft of illumination into the work and life of John Clare' who spent most of the last decades of his life in asylums for the insane. I shall argue against

---

[15] Williams, Raymond *The Country and the City,* (London, Vintage Classics, 2016), p. 204

[16] Burwick, Fredrick *Poetic Madness and the Romantic Imagination, (*Pennsylvania, Pennsylvania State University Press, p., 1996), p.1.

Jonathan Bate *John Clare* (2004)[17] that the 'heightened language' of John Clare's version of *Don Juan* composed while in Dr Allen's private asylum High Beech in Epping Forest was a product of confinement. I will rather suggest that lewd and bawdy language which has no earlier manifestation in the writing of John Clare was the product of mental illness, hypo-mania. I shall endeavour to provide primary sources both of poetry and prose to illustrate this. I will employ Sylvia Plath's late poetry as another example of challenging and manic writing. Clare *Don Juan* will be shown as a reaction to Byronism which forms the backbone of this argument, especially *Don Juan*. It is possible to perceive the tension between what Aristotle had called 'a special gift' and 'madness' in both Lord Byron's and John Clare's writing. This, interestingly, we will discern in the use of his grammar or the 'awkward squad' as John Clare called it. Particularly that which was written more directly through the lens of the social phenomena of Byronism. The latter was itself a question of class. We see John Clare as torn in many directions. I will further suggest that Jonathan Bate although correct in arguing that John Clare could write prose as well as poetry in High Beech Asylum thus disproving Clare's doctor's, Dr Allen's thesis, that he could only write poetry. However, returning to my central argument, Jonathan Bate maintains that John Clare's disturbing revisiting of *Don Juan* was the product of containment in the hospital rather that

---

[17]Bate, Jonathan. *John* Clare. (London: Picador, 2004).

of a mind in the grip of a mania. [18] But he does not address the question of the misogynistic content and the erratic punctuation here. I shall endeavour to illustrate by way of John Clare's pre-asylum writing that he could write sane poetry and prose but when writing about Lord Byron as early as 1825 (his first hospitalization was in 1838) his writing would become ungrammatical, galloping along as if in a hypo-manic state of mind. My argument will be supported by primary texts of both poetry and prose. I understand Virginia Woolf's comments on Byron's *Don Juan* as cogent:

It is the most readable poem of its length ever written... It's what one has looked for in vain-an elastic shape which will hold whatever you choose to put in it.[19]

It is possible to maintain that Byronism embodied a contradiction which is illustrated by his biographical details of libertinism and his revolutionary poetic aspirations such as in *Don Juan*:

I do not know; - I wish men to be free
As much from mobs as kings- from you and me.
Lord Byron, Don Juan, IX, 25, 7-8 [20]

The assonance of 'o's, 'e's created a sense of depth when combined with the iambs that provide

---

[18] Bate, Jonathan (2004) pp.446-450
[19] McGann, Jerome J. *Don Juan in Context* (London, John Murry, 1976) p, 10.
[20] Lord Byron, The Major Works, (Oxford, Oxford World Classics, 2008), p. 684. Hereafter DJ p. #

pace but broken by caesura which adds a hint of dark questioning and then the masculine rhyme 'ee' stressed freedom. 'Poetry demands a man with a special gift…or a touch of madness' [Aristotle, *Poetics*, 1455a][21]. In the case of Lord Byron his lines in *Lara* provide an insight, I suggest into him or at least his authorial persona, the Byronic Hero:

> His madness was not of the head, but heart;
>
> Lord Byron, Lara Canto IX, L 358 22.

That was a constant throughout Byron's poetry and prose. To encapsulate my position here, Byron was articulate to the point of genius but troubled rather than 'mad'. Byron reinforces this concept in a collection of journal entries *Detached Thoughts*:

> …at heart you are the most melancholy of mankind,[23]

The Romantic poets would have not necessarily have seen themselves as a 'school of poets'. However, they could be perceived as reacting against Neo-Classicism, the Enlightenment, and Alexander Pope. Hence, I shall explore the relationship between Byron and Alexander Pope a little deeper through a variety of

---

[21] Burwick, Fredrick (1996) p.1.
[22] Byron. Lord, *Selected Poems*, (London Penguin Classics, 2003), p.326.
[23] Byron, Lord *Selected Letters and Journals* [ed] Leslie A. Marchant, (Massachusetts, Harvard University Press, 1982), p, 275

primary texts. Here is an extract from Pope's early *Essay on Criticism:*

Those RULES of old discover'd, not devis'd,
Are Nature still, but Nature Methodiz'd;
Nature, like Liberty, is but restrain'd
By the same Laws which first herself ordain'd.
Hear how learn'd Greece her useful Rules indites,[24]

Then juxtapose this with a letter from Byron to Murray, September 15th, 1817:

With regard to poetry in general, I am convinced, the more I think of it, that he and all of us — Scott, Southey, Wordsworth, I, — are all in the wrong, one as much as another; that we are upon a wrong revolutionary system or, not worth a damn in itself, ... I am the more confirmed in this by having lately gone over some of our classics particularly Pope. Depend upon it, it is all Horace then, and Claudian now, among us; and if I had to begin again, I would model myself accordingly... [25]

Therefore, it is consistent that Byron should choose the genre employed by Alexander Pope in his major poem *The Rape of the Lock,* a mock-heroic narrative poem for his opus, *Don Juan* which is a multi-voiced or dialogic mock-satire. Thus, I show that Byron was more profoundly rooted in the Greek and Latin traditions of poetry

---

[24] Pope, Alexander *Selected Poetry* (Oxford, Oxford World Classics, 2008) p.3
[25] Marchant (1982), p. 167

than Wordsworth or Southey. I illustrate the intellectual basis of his attacks on them in the suppressed until 1834 *Dedication* to Don *Juan*. Here Byron assails Wordsworth:

And Wordsworth, in a rather long "Excursion"
(I think the quarto holds five hundred pages),
Has given a sample from the vasty version
Of his new system to perplex the sages;
'Tis poetry—at least by his assertion,
And may appear so when the dog-star rages—
And he who understands it would be able
To add a story to the Tower of Babel.
DJ, Dedication, 4 L.25-32.

I understand that Lord Byron is using Ottava Rima. In English the Ottava Rima stanza consists of eight iambic lines, usually iambic pentameters. Each stanza consists of three alternate rhymes and one double rhyme, following an ab, ab, ab, cc scheme. Thus, allowing a witty couplet on lines 7&8. I can, therefore, understand Byron's *Don Juan* as subverting Romanticism by referencing the work of Augustan poets such as Alexander Pope's satirical mock-heroic poetry. This contrasted with Wordsworth *Preface to Lyrical Ballads,* 1802 which advocated the use of ordinary language about the masses but transmuted through the mind of a quasi-divine power, the Poet. The differentiation of Neo-Classical and Romantic poetry had been referred to by W. H. Abrams as the 'mirror' and 'lamp.'[26]. Pre-Romantic

---

[26]Abrams W, H. *The Mirror and the Lamp: Romantic Theory and the Critical Tradition* (Oxford, Oxford

poetry was understood as a mirror and Romantic illuminated through a 'lamp'. Thus, the genre that he decided to write within was particularly significant. He almost taunts his reader as towards the end of his mock-epic-satire informed them exactly what they had been reading:

And I shall take a much more serious air
Than I have yet done in this epic satire.
DJ, Canto XIV, 99, 790-792.

Air/satire rhymed teasingly with a tumbling enjambment. Then he confronted the reader with:

Is strange-but true; for Truth is always strange,
Stranger than Fiction: if it could be told,
DJ, Canto XIV, 101, 801-803.

Byron's intellect and creativity were toying with the reader. The reader had just been given concrete generic information by Byron, then left to ponder. What is true? What is Fiction? Yet Byron had written to John Murray, August 21st, 1821

> Almost all of Don Juan is real life-either my own-or from people I knew.[27]

Of course, although the genre is epic-satire that does not mean *Don Juan* is merely a protracted swipe at those institutions Lord Byron disapproved

---

University Press 1971}
[27] Marchant, Leslie, (1982). p, 256.

of. He was writing in a narrative of poetry. For as T.S. Eliot noted in *The Sacred Wood:*

No poet, no artist of any art, has his complete meaning alone His significance, his appreciation is the appreciation of his relation to the dead poets and artists. You cannot value him alone; you must set him, for contrast and comparison, among the dead.[28]

I would now like to comment on the Don Juan legend more generally. Moyra Haslett, a leading Byron scholar, noted a looseness in Don Juan as a legend which originated in 1630 with the tragic drama *The Trickster of Seville and the Stone Guest* attributed to a Spanish monk, Tirso de Molina. Therefore, one can conclude that Byron was allowing himself ample literary space for a 'writing back' when he chose the Don Juan legend:

The legend of the Don Juan was never intrinsically partisan. Indeed, it could be appropriated for contrary arguments and indeed, its ambivalent political status has enabled many political readings.[29]

Although, that is not to argue that Byron was not committed to a progressive belief-system, merely that his class orientation was not objectively opposed to capitalism as in the case of the

---

[28] Eliot, T.S. *The Sacred Wood*, (London, Faber & Faber, 1997) p.41

[29] Haslett, Moyra, *Byron's Don Juan and the Don Juan Legend* (Oxford, Clarendon Press 2003), p.176.

interests of proletarians or systematically organized in terms of ideas as in the case of Shelley. When his publisher Murray wanted to suppress parts of *Don Juan* Byron wrote back with some conviction: 'I will not give way to all the Cant of Christendom.'[30] Here is the crux for Byron as he believed 'Cant' or hypocrisy was prevalent in the society he placed his contribution to the *Don Juan* narrative within. Byron's *Don Juan* was as mentioned a powerful 'writing back' to Tirso de Molina *The Trickster of Serville and the Stone Guest*, 1630 but also to Mozart's opera with the libretto by Lorenzo da Ponte *Don Giovanni*. Don Juan in both of these was the seducer rather than the seduced. However, Byron turns both the drama and the opera on its head with the women acting as seductresses. The women are powerful in a manner that was quite radical for the British reading public at the beginning of the nineteenth century and echoes Geoffrey Chaucer's *The Wife of Bath's Tale* in *The Canterbury Tales*, 1404-1410. As Moyra Haslett correctly argued, class matters:

Because of his social position as a member of the ruling class in decay, Don Juan carried out Jacobinism in the only field open to him – that of sexuality.[31]

Nevertheless, she also maintained that:
However, this 'revolutionary' sexual behaviour

---

[30] Leslie A. Marchant (1982), p.328.
[31] Haslett, Moyra (2003). p.185.

is gendered. Women could hardly avail themselves without incurring severe penalties and the degree to which they benefited from such activity is questionable.[32]

I would rather understand Byron's treatment of women in *Don Juan* as empowering because he had inverted the legend and thus the patriarchal relations involved in the original versions mentioned by Tirso de Molina and Mozart. Thus, we can comprehend two essential components for my analysis: class and gender and I would argue in agreement with Frederick Engels:

According to the materialist conception of history, the ultimately determining element in history is the production and reproduction of real life. Other than this neither Marx nor I have ever asserted...[33]

We have understood why Byron made caustic attacks on Wordsworth and Coleridge. Indeed, there was also a degree of personal acrimony, but class hostility was key between the 'Grasmere scribblers' to use Byron's phrase regarding Wordsworth and Coleridge but also the younger Romantic poets like Keats who suggested rather peevishly to his brother:

You speak of Lord Byron and me – There is this great difference between us. He

---

[32] Haslett, Moyra (2003) p.186,
[33] Marx, Karl & Engels, Frederick, *Selected Correspondence* (Moscow, Progress Publishers, 1965) p, 417-419

describes what he sees – I describe what I imagine – Mine is the hardest task.[34]

Nevertheless, Byron's attacks on leading figures in the British politico-military complex such as Wellington and Castlereagh were strident and caustic attacks on the oppressor nation and the futility of war. It is significant that unlike Wordsworth and Coleridge, Byron had not been a young man in the heady days of the French Revolution. As the young William Wordsworth wrote:

Oh! Pleasant exertion of hope and joy!

For mighty were the auxiliars which there stood

Upon our side, we were strong in love!

Bliss it was to be alive,

But to be young was very heaven![35]

    Both Wordsworth and Coleridge, all the Grasmere Poets would retreat into reaction as reaction established itself both in Europe and the British Isles after this period of revolutionary tumult. Nevertheless, an uprising in Ireland, the United Irishmen, in 1798, led by the Protestant Wolfe Tone had been brutally suppressed on the orders of Lord Castlereagh and he also organised state repression in England, notably the Peterloo

---

[34] Keats, John, *Selected Letters* (London, Penguin Books, 2014) p, 427.

[35] https://www.poetryfoundation.org/.../the-french-revolution-as-it-appeared-to-enthusia.

Massacre of 1819. Although Castlereagh committed suicide in 1822, he remained a figure of hatred in progressive circles and amongst the poor. Shelley wrote a scathing poem after the Peterloo Massacre in Manchester *The Masque of Anarchy*[36]. There is no hint of satire in Byron's attacks on Castlereagh. Here in the Dedication *Don Juan* he invokes and references the seventeenth-century revolutionary poet John Milton who spoke of being 'fallen in evil days on evil tongues' *Paradise Lost Bk 7, L.25* after the defeat of the English Revolution:

If, fallen in evil days on evil tongues,

Milton appeal'd to the Avenger, Time,

DJ. Dedication, X. l 72-73.

Would he adore a sultan? he obey

The intellectual eunuch Castlereagh?

Dedication, XI, l 87-88.

Byron's assault on Castlereagh does not in the slightest resemble the satirical, its biting lines contrast with the concluding mock-satire of the English Cantos of *Don Juan* which Byron did not complete because of his premature death. It is

---

[36] See Paul Foot *Red Shelley* (London, Sidgwick & Jackson, 1980) for a cogent Marxist analysis of Percy Bysshe
 Shelley and his epoch.

rather an attack on a hated symbol of oppression. Here again, we saw a divide in Byron between the revolutionary and satirist. Byron made blistering attacks on Castlereagh's repression in Ireland:

Cold-blooded, smooth-faced, placid miscreant!

Dabbling its sleek young hands in Erin's blood.

Lines 88-90 are shocking, and they impacted on the masses as Richard Lansdown argued:

And it was Don Juan that working people read. At the Great Chartist demonstration held at Newcastle on 27th June 1838, several banners carried quotes from

Byron's epic poem DJ, 671-2, for example:

'REVOLLUTION

I have seen some nations, like o'er load asses,

Kick off their burdens, meaning the high classes.'

By 1838, Byron's poetry had entered what historian

William St. Clair calls 'the radical canon' of the nineteenth

century working class.[37]

---

[37] Lansdown Richard, The Cambridge Introduction to Byron (Cambridge, Cambridge University Press,
   2012). P. 158.

Marx was aware though of the limitations of poets like Byron and the strengths of those like Shelley:

The real difference between Byron and Shelley is this:

those who understand them and love them rejoice that Byron died at thirty-six, because if he had lived, he would have become a reactionary bourgeois; they grieve that Shelley died at twenty-nine, because he was essentially a revolutionist, and he would always have been one of the advanced guard of Socialism.[38]

We have comprehended a 'class' element in Byron's assault on William Wordsworth who was not a member of the aristocracy and John Keats referred to as 'the cockney poet.' Byron had also made an attack on a successful 'labourer poet' Robert Bloomfield and his brother Nathan in *English Bards and Scottish Reviewers*:

Lo! Burns and Bloomfield, nay, a greater far,

Gifford was born beneath an adverse star,

Forsook the labours of a servile state,

Stemm'd the rude storm, and triumph'd over fate:

Then why no more? if Phœbus smiled on you,

Bloomfield! why not on brother Nathan too?

Him to the mania, not the muse, has seized;

---

[38] Marx, Karl & Engels, Frederick, On Literature and Art (Moscow, Progress Publishers 1976) pp. 320- 21.

Not inspiration, but a mind diseased:[39]

The final couplet above illustrates an unpleasantly caustic and patronizing attitude of Byron's towards 'labourer poets' and indeed, those of them who became mentally ill. It illuminates that contradiction within Byron but also those of his objective class interests and those of the poets from the rural poor like John Clare and Robert Bloomfield. Thus, we can see an element of hypocrisy in Byron who in *Don Juan* attacked the 'Cant' of the ruling elite of Britain at the time while he had indulged in a similar orientation. Christopher Caudwell noted in his early Marxian study into British poetics:

Byron is an aristocrat – but he is one conscious of the break-up of his class as a force, and the necessity to go over to the bourgeoisie. Hence his mixture of cynicism and romanticism.[40]

John Clare wrote these poignant lines towards the end of his life while compulsorily detained in Northampton County Lunatic Asylum:

I am - yet what I am, none care or knows;

My friends forsake me like a memory lost:

I am the self-consumer of my woes –

---

[39] Lord Byron *Selected Poems*, (2003). P.36 L. 777-784.

[40] Caudwell, Christopher, *Illusion and Reality* (London, Lawrence & Wishart, 1977) p, 104.

They rise and vanish in oblivion's host.

John Clare: Lines: 'I am'[41]

Two pieces of prose here illustrated John Clare's ambivalent relationship with grammar. This is an area of Clare scholarship which is addressed in, at least, two sources exclusively as well as marginally in other texts. See especially:

a) Eluding the Awkward Squad: John Clare's Punctuation, The Absence of

    Punctuation in John Clare's Sonnet *'Field Thoughts'*, Martyn Crucefix.[42]

b) *John Clare and the Tyranny of Grammar*, James C. McKusick.[43]

However, for my purposes I wish to delineate the relationship and connections between John Clare's perspective on grammar and his use of it in two rare prose pieces and then apply these findings to his revisiting of Byron's *Don Juan*. John Clare's poem reveals more than just an uncertain use of grammar but will be shown to employ a heightened libidinal language which descends into pushing the boundaries of acceptability which is not present elsewhere in John Clare's writing. I will argue against Jonathan Bate when he maintained that this was the product of mere confinement rather that of a mind in the grip of a mania:

---

[41] Clare, John *Selected Poems* [ed] Bate, Jonathan, (London, Faber & Faber, 2005), p.282.
[42] www.pnreview.co.uk/cgi-bin/scribe?item_id=8675
[43] http://www.jstor.org/stable/25601059

Jonathan Bate does not address the question of bawdy language and punctuation here. Rather two examples of John Clare's prose are useful as a beginning in understanding his relationship with grammar or 'awkward squad' as John Clare defined it. This piece of prose was composed in 1821 but not published until 1931:

'Grammar' [...]

I thought sometimes that I surely had a taste peculiarly by myself and that nobody else thought or saw things as I did. I pursued my literary journey as usual, working hard all day and scribbling at night, or any leisure hour, in any convenient hole or corner I could shove in unseen; for I always carried a pencil in my pocket. Till necessity, as I got up towards manhood, urged me to look for something more than pleasing one's self, my poems had been kept with the greatest industry under wish'd concealment. The laughs and jeers of those around me, when they found out I was a poet, was present death to my ambitious apprehensions; for in our unlettered villages, the best of the inhabitants have little more knowledge in reading than what can be gleaned from a weekly Newspaper, Old Moore's Almanack, and a Prayer Book...[44]

---

[44] Williams Merryn and Raymond Clare, *John. John Clare: Selected Poetry and Prose* (Routledge English Texts)
(Kindle Locations 1040-1060). Taylor and Francis. Kindle Edition.

This example shows a knowledge of grammar. Another piece of prose is devoid of grammar and gallops along at a tremendous rate, it is essentially three pages of unpunctuated observation and comment entitled, *Byron's Funeral* [45]. This is of interest in-itself as it suggests a relationship established long before John Clare's collapse into mental illness between erratic writing and Byronism. It was written in 1825 but not published until 1951. I note that this is concluded with lines which illustrated John Clare's 'class' orientation as well as the lack of punctuation:

I believe that his liberal principals in religion & politics did a great deal towards gaining the notice & affections of the lower orders be as it will it is better to be beloved by those low & humble for undisguised honesty then flattered by the great for purchased & pensiond hypocrisy – [...][46]

The second continues in the same misogynistic vein Care (*Don Juan*, p168). He appeared deranged. As Williams (1986, p.242) noted correctly: 'It is dominated by a bitterness towards

---

[45] Williams Merryn & Raymond Clare, John. John Clare: Selected Poetry and Prose (Routledge English Texts)
    (Kindle Locations 3138-3167). Taylor and Francis. Kindle Edition.
[46] Williams Merryn & Raymond Clare, John. John Clare: Selected Poetry and Prose (Routledge English Texts,
    (Kindle Locations 3163-3165). Taylor and Francis. Kindle Edition.

women (as in Shakespeare's darker plays) for which there is no obvious reason.' It is written in Ottava Rima but with what Jonathan Bate (2004) called 'outrageous rhymes.'

My position is that by this time John Clare was an established poet, he knew the craft but was 'manic' as Sylvia Plath was when she wrote *Daddy*. That contained the memorable and mould-breaking:

> Daddy, daddy, you bastard, I am through.[47]

Sylvia Plath was in a state of elevated mood which oscillated with depression that concluded in suicide. She wrote in a patriarchal society that oppressed her. John Clare did reference class oppression in *Don Juan*:

I wish M. P's. would spin less yarn – no doubt

But burn false bills and cross bad taxes out

Clare, Don Juan, p.169.

However, the sexism extending to hatred is almost inexplicable in John Clare's poem. The key to understanding it is the lack of end-stops in his *Don Juan*. I had previously shown when writing about Lord Byron his grammar and punctuation became erratic. He was in a manic state in which sexuality can be distorted and elevated. We understand John Clare as torn by Gramscian 'contradictory consciousness', alienation from the poor and

---

[47] Plath, Sylvia *Ariel* (London, Faber & Faber, 1965), p.56

intelligentsia and manic. Thus, the poetry becomes warped and without punctuation as refracted through the mind-bending prism of Byronic libertinism for as Marx argued:

> The ideas of the ruling class are in every epoch, the ruling ideas.[48]

I understand Byronism as a cultural manifestation of the dominant ideology of its epoch which was one of transition and Clare's *Don Juan* as being distorted by the former because of the uneven class relationships. In the last instance though, John Clare did not find a 'voice' that would withstand the pressures of capitalism. Rather his voice became overwhelmed by the dominant ideology and a slanted version of Byronism. John Clare would live, writing profusely, in asylums largely forgotten by the literary world and society. Both Byron and Clare belonged to classes which would either come to an accord or be assimilated into the contending classes of modernity, the bourgeoisie and the proletariat respectively. Only the latter can create communism and the conditions for a new poetic because as Marx had argued persuasively:

> The revolution cannot take poetry from the past only the future.[49]

---

[48] Marx & Engels (1982) p.64.
[49]
https://www.marxists.org/archive/marx/works/1852/18th-brumaire/ch01.htm

Bibliography.

Primary Sources.

Bloomfield, Robert, *Selected Poems* [ed] Goodridge, J & Lucas, J (Nottingham, Trent Editions, 2007).

Byron, Lord. *Byron's Letters and Journals: A New Selection* [ed] Landsdown, Richard (Oxford, Oxford University Press, 2015).

Byron, Lord, *Selected Letters and Journals* [ed] Leslie A. Marchant, (Massachusetts, Harvard University Press, 1982).

Byron, Lord, *The Major Works,* [ed] McGann, Jerome, J (Oxford, Oxford World Classics, 2008).

Byron, Lord, *Selected Poems,* [ed] Wolfson, Susan J and Manning, Peter (London Penguin Classics, 2003).

Clare, John, *Selected Poems* [ed] Bate, Jonathan, (London, Faber & Faber, 2005).

Clare, John, *Poems selected by Paul Farley* (London, Faber & Faber, 2007).

Clare, John, *By Himself* [ed] Robinson, E & Powell, D (Manchester Carcanet Books, 2002).

Clare, John, *Major Works,* [ed] Robinson, E & Powell, D (Oxford, Oxford University Press, 2008).

Clare, John, *Selected Poetry and Prose [ed],* Williams, Merryn & Raymond (London, Methuen, 1986).

Clare, John, *The Letters of John Clare* [ed] Storey, Mark (Oxford, Oxford University Press, 2014).

Keats, John, *Selected Letters* [ed] Bernard, John (London, Penguin Books, 2014).

Keats, John, *The Complete Poems* [ed] Bernard, John (London, Penguin Classics, 1988).

Pope, Alexander, *Selected Poems* [ed] Rogers, Pat (Oxford, Oxford University Press, 2008).

Shelley, Percy Bysshe, *The Major Works* [ed] Leader, Zachary & O'Neill, Michael (Oxford, Oxford University Press, 2009).

Wordsworth, William, *The Major Works* [ed] Gill, Stephen (Oxford, Oxford University Press, 2008).

Secondary Sources.

Abrams W, H. *The Mirror and the Lamp: Romantic Theory and the Critical Tradition* (Oxford, Oxford University Press, 1971).

Barrell, John, *The Idea of Landscape and the sense of Place 1730-1840, An approach to the poetry of John Clare*. (Cambridge, Cambridge University Press, 2010).

Bate, Jonathan. *John Clare.* (London: Picador, 2004).

Lord Byron's Don Juan: Modern Critical Interpretations [ed] Bloom, Harold (New York, Harold Chelsea House Publishers, 1987).

Bone, Drummond, *Byron Writers and their Work* (Northcote House, British Council, 2000).

The Cambridge Companion to Byron [ed] Bone, Drummond (Cambridge, Cambridge University Press, 2004).

Byron: The Poetry of Politics and Politics of Poetry [ed] Beaton, Roderick & Kenton-Jones, Christine (London, Routledge, 2017).

Burwick, Fredrick, *Poetic Madness and the Romantic Imagination,* (Pennsylvania, Pennsylvania State University Press, 1996).

Caudwell, Christopher, *Illusion and Reality* (London, Lawrence & Wishart, 1977).

The Cambridge Companion to British Romantic Poetry [ed] Chandler, James & McLane, M Maureen (Cambridge, Cambridge University Press, 2008).

Eliot, T.S. *The Sacred Wood*, (London, Faber & Faber, 1997).

Foot, Paul, *Red Shelley* (London, Sidgwick & Jackson, 1980).

Franklin, Caroline, *Byron* (London, Routledge, 2007).

Gramsci, Antonio, *Selections from the Prison Notebooks*, (New York, International Publishers Co; Reprint, 1989 edition (November 24, 1971).

John Clare in Context [ed] Haughton, Hugh, Philips, Adam and Summerfield, Geoffrey, (Cambridge, Cambridge University Press, 2005)

Haslett, Moyra, *Byron's Don Juan and the Don Juan Legend* (Oxford, Clarendon Press, 2003).

Haslett, Moyra, *Marxist Literary and Cultural Theories (Transitions)* (Basingstoke, Palgrave Macmillan, 2000).

Heywood, Andrew, *Political Ideas and Concepts: An Introduction, (London*, Macmillan,1994).

Byron Childe Harold's Pilgrimage and Don Juan: a casebook [ed] Jump, John (London, Macmillan Press Ltd, 1973)

Lacas, John, Clare Writers and their Work (Northcote House, British Council, 1994).

The Cambridge Introduction to Byron [ed] Lansdown, Richard, (Cambridge, Cambridge University Press, 2012).

A Companion to Romantic Poetry [ed] Mahoney, Charles, (Chichester, Wiley-Blackwell, 2011).

MacCarthy, Fiona, *Byron Life and Legend*. (London, John Murray, 2004).

McGann, Jerome J. *Byron and Romanticism* (Cambridge, Cambridge University Press, 2002).

McGann, Jerome J. *Don Juan in Context* (London, John Murry, 1976).

Marx, Karl & Engels, Frederick, *On Literature and Art* (Moscow, Progress Publishers 1976).

Marx, Karl & Engels, Frederick *The Communist Manifesto* (Harmondsworth, Penguin Books, 1976).

Marx, Karl & Engels, Frederick, The *German Ideology* (London, Lawrence & Wishart,1982).

Marx, Karl & Engels, Frederick, *Selected Correspondence* (Moscow, Progress Publishers, 1965).

Plath, Sylvia, *Ariel* (London, Faber & Faber, 1965).

Robertson, R, *Mock-Epic Poetry from Pope to Heine* (Oxford, Oxford University Press, 2009).

Byron: The Critical Heritage [ed] Rutherford, Andrew, (London, Routledge & Kegan Paul, 1970).

Stabler, Jane, *Byron* (London, Longman, 1998).

St. Clair, William, *The Reading Nation in the Romantic Period,* (Cambridge, Cambridge University Press, 2007).

Storey. Mark, *The Poetry of John Clare: A critical introduction* (London, Macmillan, 1974).

Clare, J, The Critical Heritage [ed] Storey, Mark (London, Routledge & Kegan Paul, 1973).

Thompson, E. P. *The Making of the English Working Class*, (London, Penguin Books, 1991).

Vardy, Alan, John Clare, Politics and Poetry (Basingstoke, Palgrave Macmillan, 2003).

White, Adam, *John Clare's Romanticism* (Switzerland, Palgrave Macmillan, 2017).

Robert Bloomfield: Lyric, Class and the Romantic Canon [ed] White, Simon, Goodridge, John and Keegan, Bridge (Lewisburg, Bucknell University Press, 2006).

Williams, Raymond, *Culture and Materialism: Selected Essays* (Verso, London, 2005).

Williams, Raymond, *The Country and the City* (London, Vintage Classics, 2016).

Williams, Raymond, *The Long Revolution* (London, Chatto & Windus Ltd, 1961).

Don Juan Theory in Practice [ed] Wood, Nigel, (Buckingham, Open University Press, 1995).

Milton and Blake.

I firstly suggest that, Milton *Paradise Lost* (1674), because of the material circumstances in which it was written, those of the defeat of the English Revolution, must have limited the capacity for human freedom as it was a poem born of defeat. The defeat of the first bourgeois revolution humanity had experienced. Whereas in Blake's poetry and we understand that he was writing in a period of revolutionary upturn, principally the French Revolution. Thus, a period of hope rather than despair for the masses because of the potential for greater human freedom:

Rouze up O Young Men of the New Age! set your foreheads against the ignorant Hirerings! For we have Hirerings in the camp, the Court, & the University: who would if they could for ever depress Mental and prolong Corporeal War. Blake, *Milton,* 1, 11-15. 50

Having delineated a general conceptual orientation for my argument in regard of human freedom in Milton and in Blake's poetry which will be elaborated upon. I secondly argue for a complexified reading of the relationship between the poet and society founded on a correct understanding of dialectical materialism as suggested by Leon Trotsky[51] is necessary in the

---

[50] Blake, William, *The Complete Poems* [ed] Ostriker, *Alicia* (London, Penguin Classics, 2004), p 513.
[51] Leon, Trotsky, *Art and Revolution: Writings on Literature, Politics and Culture* (New York, Pathfinder, 2013).

last instance. I hence suggest, therefore, that in this context, reductionist arguments: economic, psychoanalytical or otherwise are inadequate to totally explain the genius of poets like Dante, Milton and Blake.

When the reader approaches any text the question of genre immediately arises. *PL* was in some ways a contradiction, an epic that transcended the epic form. It addresses the heart of Western civilisation especially in the pre-modern, even now in a post meta-narrative post-modernity world *PL* has relevance, the Fall and Redemption. The Biblical account contained little depth for Adam or Eve, this Milton attempted to remedy in *PL* and he also addressed the 'Problem of Evil.' So, we understand Milton using a Homeric and pagan form, the epic, addressed the questions of Christianity, but we see him doing it at a concrete moment in history:

Anger and just rebuke, and judgement give'n
That brought into this world a world of woe,
Death's harbinger: sad task, yet argument
Not less but more heroic than the wrath
Of stern Achilles... [52]

It is also important to ground *PL* in the Reformation. This brought, amongst Protestants, the rejection of a complex biblical scholarship known as the 'Fourfold Method' and a return to one manifestation of biblical literalism, probably

---

[52] Milton, John, *Paradise Lost* [ed] Leonard, John, (London, Penguin Classics, 2003). BK IX, L 10-14, Hereafter *PL* Bk #

more complex than that practiced by Evangelical Protestants today though, with a method called 'typology'. This can be comprehended as type=type, thus Adam, the first man at Creation and Jesus Christ the Son of God who was understood to be the new or substitute Adam, for a new age, were the same 'type'. The New Testament was translated by John Tyndale into English, who had paid with his life. It then became inevitable that eventually a mass produced, and state authorized version would become available. This occurred in 1611 with the *King James Version*. The Bible had become the site of ideological contestation for Protestants. I would go further than Christopher Hill's arguments and argue it became a handbook of revolution, a text which challenged the priestly secrecy of the Latin *Vulgate Bible,* the Divine Right of the monarch and advocated the Kingdom of God on Earth for the poor in *Luke 6: 20-21* in the 'common tongue' or at least an accessible language:

> Blessed are ye poor:
>
> yours is the kingdom of God:
>
> Blessed are ye who hunger:
>
> ye shall be filled.[53]

I would comment, that the use of the English language in the *King James Version* as a literary text has enthralled writers and readers over the

---

[53] The Bible: Authorized King James version with Apocrypha, *St. Luke*, (Oxford, Oxford World's Classics, 1997), p.80

centuries, it remains the essential or 'master narrative' of English literature and has seen writing back from most significant authors. Christopher Hill maintained:

That the Bible was, or should be, the foundation of all English cultures.

On this principle, most Protestants agreed. If we do not grasp this we are slipping into an anachronistic trap.[54] I would like to stress the position taken by W. R. Owens[55] For our purposes, however, we take the Bible to be a product of human history and culture, and as such open to analysis and exploration from many standpoints. This approach should not be taken as implying any lack of respect towards those who regard it as the Word of God.

Milton had adhered to two radical seventeenth-century heresies both can be located in *De Doctrina Christiana* which was not discovered until 1823 and published in 1825 and is still contested by some as not Milton's work. They are Arminianism and Arianism. The former, which understood human beings to have complete 'Free Will'. Hence being an ideologue, he placed his theology in the mouth of the Christian God in *PL,*

---

[54] Christopher Hill, *The English Bible and the Seventeenth Century Revolution (London, Allen Lane, The Penguin Press,* (1993). P 7.

[55] Owens, W. R. *A815 MA English Course Reader. Part 2 Paradise Lost* (Milton Keynes, The Open University, 2009), p. 4.

his understanding of the nature of The Fall in *Genesis 3.22:*

> And the Lord God said, Behold,
> the man is become as one of us,
> to know good and evil: and now, lest he put
> forth his hand, and take also of the tree of life,
> and eat, and live for ever.[56]

The desire for humanity to attain Divinity:

> I made him just and right,
> Sufficient to have stood, though free to fall…
>
> as if predestination overruled
>
> There will, disposed by absolute decree
>
> Of high foreknowledge, they themselves decreed
>
> Their own revolt not I,
>   (*PL*, BK III. L 99-117).

Here Milton used onomatopoeia in L 100, the reader feels as if they are also falling 'free to fall'. However, the rejoinder came from Adam, not Satan and is both potent and poignant as he makes a counter-accusation in his postlapsarian condition and echoes the cries of an alienated humanity across history; 'why me?':

Did I request thee, Maker, from my clay

---

[56] The Bible (1997) *Genesis*, p. 4

To mould me man, did I solicit thee

From darkness to promote me, or here place

In this delicious garden?

   (PL, Bk X 743-45).

The assonance of 'a', 'y' 'o' and 'e' sound in combination with the alliterative 'm's give an urgency which flows like a torrent of anguish from Adam's mouth while the caesura after 'me' L. 744 followed with the overflowing and despairing enjambment of L 744-45., suggest an almost Lucifer like defiance, but it is human authenticity and created pathos. Hence, I argue that Adam rather than Satan is the poetic agent who challenges Milton's intended aspiration 'to justify the ways of God to man', (*PL* Bk 1,26.)

   The latter of Milton's two heretical positions Arianism, which importantly saw the Father Deity separate and existing before his Son, Jesus Christ. There is simply little trace of omnibenevolence, given the Father's omniscience. Recollecting that Milton was an Arminian we do not read him as privileging the Son of God's necessary, in Christian iconography, sacrifice of the crucifixion, the latter is almost written out of *PL* as noted by Professor John Carey. Carey argued that this invalidates the poem as a Christian poem.[57] He continued:

---

[57] Carey, John, *The Essential Paradise Lost* (London, Faber & Faber, 2017) p.229-232.

If the Son- just once- burst out with an expression of his love for mankind when he saw how beautiful humans were, as Satan does, it would transform the whole poem. But he never does.[58]

John Carey might have been stretching a point here because *PL* is self-evidently a Christian poem.

Milton as argued by Christopher Hill[59] P*L* was written in a period of defeat of the English Revolution by a disappointed and blind revolutionary millennialist. He regarded the epoch as one of Satanic reaction, The Restoration of the monarchy in the form of Charles II as here:

> though fall'n on evil days,
>
> On evil days though fall'n, and evil tongues;
>
> In darkness, and with dangers compassed round,
>
> And solitude; yet not alone, while thou
>
> Visit'st my slumbers Nightly, or when Morn
>
> Purples the East: still govern thou my Song,
>
> Urania, and fit audience find, though few.
>
> (*P L* Book VII 25-30).

He was alone but for his Muse who is identified by implication as the Holy Spirit *PL* BK1, but is also

---

[58] Carey (2017) p.232.
[59] Hill, Christopher, *Milton and the English Revolution* (London, Faber & Faber, 1977).

referred to as Urania, the Muse of Astronomy. On this count, it is worth recollecting that the young Milton visited the aged Galileo. His Muse and a few comrades and family to whom he dictated the text were in fear of mobs of drunken Royalists. The use of alliteration with 'f' sounds in L 30-32 creates an ethereal sense in Milton's writing, but the reader was then confronted in L 32-33 with the:

> barbarous dissonance Of Bacchus.

Fredrick Engels reminded us: 'Let us not forget Milton, the first defender of regicide'[60]. Thus, as suggested, following the seminal work of Christopher Hill, we understand the overarching socio-historical perspective for this epic poem was the defeat of the English Revolution. The contribution Christopher Hill has made in positioning *PL* in concrete material conditions cannot be exaggerated. Christopher Hill, *The English Bible and the Seventeenth Century Revolution (*1993) made a pertinent observation:

> Englishmen had to face a totally unexpected revolutionary situation in the 1640s and 1650s, with no theoretical guidance such as Rousseau or Marx gave to their French and Russian successors, and no experience of any previous event that had been called a revolution. They had to improvise. The Bible in English was

---

[60] Engels, Frederick *The Northern Star,* 18th December 1847.

the book to which they naturally turned for guidance.[61]

Nevertheless, Christopher Hill's work had generally failed to take its revolutionary implications to their logical conclusion, that of a modern revolution. This can be explained because historians like Christopher Hill and E. P. Thompson accepted the post-war 'historical compromise' with western capitalism that had been argued for by some Marxists. Thus, these theoreticians had very real limitations when addressing the question of human freedom as a concept which embraced revolutionary praxis. They could not understand that the dialectic and therefore irresolvable contradiction was not merely an abstraction, but as Marx had argued was rooted in the everyday practices of people. It should be noted that Karl Marx regarded Milton as an 'unproductive labourer' in that he did not intend to make money from *PL's* production. Rather, Marx argued: 'Milton produced *Paradise Lost* for the same reason a silk worm produces silk. It was an activity of his nature.'[62] We, therefore, need to revisit and reassess the contribution of more overtly *orthodox* Marxist literary critics such as Alick West *Crisis and Criticism & Literary Essays* (1975) and Christopher Caudwell *Illusion* and *Reality* (1977) and radical currents that emerged from feminist writers.

---

[61] Hill, Christopher, (1993), *p.9.*
[62] Marx, Karl, *Theories of Surplus Value, vol 1* (Moscow, Progress Publishers, 1969), p.401.

I shall now describe and assess two very different accounts of aesthetics and Milton from British orthodox Marxist critics Alick West and Christopher Caudwell. Firstly, Alick West[63] gave an unusual view of literature which had Freudian as well as Marxist origins. He largely understood literature as a form of positive energy or libido in the sense of Eros competing with the death wish, Thanatos. But here his convergence with Freud ended. Maynard Solomon argued this was because Alick West saw this 'energy' as rooted in material collectivises such as social class 'whereas Freud does not consistently recognize the cooperative and communistic roots of Eros, nor the class nature of Thanatos.'[64] Thus we can perceive Alick West offering a very different account to the official Socialist Realist 'line'. He was therefore in an obscure fashion closer to the original tradition of Karl Marx who had rejected 'tendentious literature' as an artistic expression. His reading of *PL* was symptomatic of his general perspective. Therefore, Heaven served as a symbol of declining feudalism [Thanatos] and the Garden of Eden as one of an emergent capitalism that humanity would be expelled from until communism created a collective Eden, maybe a garden of love, of Eros. Alick West was a tormented man because of unrelenting self

---

[63] Bounds, Philip, British Communism & the politics of Literature 1928-1939, (Pontypool, Merlin Press, 2012) pp.105-107

[64] Solomon, Maynard, *Marxism and Art* (Detroit, Wayne State University Press, 1979), p.495.

psycho-analysis. This dominated him to the detriment of his understanding of Marxism.

Christopher Caudwell argued that the bourgeois revolution in England had inevitably 'gone too far' for the bourgeoisie because their demand for unfettered freedom must unleash a massive upsurge of what he called the 'have-nots'. He suggested a 'Cromwell or a Robespierre' would be produced to temper the rebellion of the masses. To the genuinely revolutionary element, he argued, the petty-bourgeois, this was the ultimate betrayal of their revolution. Thus, he concluded:

> Therefore, in *Paradise Lost* Milton sees himself as Satan overwhelmed and yet still courageous: damned and yet revolutionary.[65]

Christopher Caudwell might here be recollecting:
Better to reign in Hell, than serve in Heav'n.
(*PL* BK 1, L 163).

He was positioning himself in the literary current that Shelley had advocated when he had argued: 'Milton's Devil as a moral being is far superior to his God.'[66]

As the seventeenth-century English revolution was not mature because of the lack of a proletariat. Therefore, following this first strand of

---

[65] Caudwell, Christopher, *Illusion and Reality* (London, Lawrence & Wishart, 1977) p. 94.
[66] Shelley, Percy Bysshe, *The Major Works* (Oxford, Oxford University Press, 2009), p.692.

my argument, the prerequisites for solving the question of patriarchy could not be addressed in a satisfactory manner. We can read Virginia Woolf describing 'the Milton bogey' in *A Room of One's Own (2002)* that has haunted and distorted women writers. Thus, we read Sandra M. Gilbert and Susan Gubar (1979):

Hence Milton himself – the real patriarchal spectre, one more bogey created by Milton: his inferior and Satanically inspired Eve, who has intimidated women and blocked their view of possibilities both real and literary...Both he (Milton) and the creatures of his imagination constitute the misogynistic essence of what Gertrude Stein called 'patriarchal poetry.'[67]

The contemporary scholar Mary Nyquist, *The Genesis of Gendered Subjectivity in the Source Traits and in Paradise Lost, (1987)* is persuasive. She correctly argues that there are two creation narratives in Genesis, firstly the 'P' account of creation in Genesis1.27 which she argued suggested something akin to a 'spiritual equality' between the sexes ('male and female created he them') and 'J' which favours patriarchy, 'where the man is created first, of the dust of the ground, with the woman being created out of his rib (Genesis, 2.7,22). Mary Nyquist continues that in Milton's 'divorce tracts the 'J' account is to be understood

---

[67] Sandra M. Gilbert and Susan Gubar: *The Madwoman in the Attic: The Woman Writers and the*

  Nineteenth- century Literary Imagination (New Haven, Conn, Yale University Press, 1979) p.188

as offering a kind of commentary on the 'P' account, which it fills out and completes.' That in *PL* vii 519–48, he splices together the 'P' and 'J' accounts in a fashion which favouring the 'J' account, in a manner, that 'specifies the gendered Adam of Paradise Lost as the "man" who is made in the divine image[68]'. This she indicates was a reflex of an emergent patriarchal capitalism where the 'public sphere' would be that of the male and the 'private' family sphere that of the woman. Therefore, she concluded John Milton was not a 'proto-feminist'. However, why is orthodox Marxist criticism valuable in this light, one good reason is its conviction that:

The change in a historical epoch can always be determined by the progress of women toward freedom, because in relation of woman to man, of the weak to the strong, the victory of human nature over brutality is most evident. The degree of emancipation of woman is the natural measure of general emancipation.[69]

Alexandra Kollontai argued that only a total restructuring of the family under communism was the solution for an emancipation of the majority of women. She recognized that bourgeois women could and would make gains under capitalism. Alexandra Kollontai suggested:

---

[68] Owens, W. R. (2009) pp. 22-3.
[69] Marx, Karl & Engels, Frederick, *The Holy Family* (Moscow, Foreign Languages Publishing House,
    1956), p, 258-59.

In place of the old individualist and egotistic family, there will rise a universal family of workers, in which all the workers, men and women, will be, above all workers, comrades.[70]

We have seen that Milton had been an early advocate of divorce but his orientation in early capitalism would have inhibited his views in the context of my initial argument. John Milton's reading of *Genesis* which he developed in *PL* with a vain and narcissistic prelapsarian Eve tempted by the prospect of becoming a 'human goddess' Bk IX, L 712 by Satan. She had already fallen in love with her own reflection BK IV L, 460-470. Eve, in Milton *PL*, also consciously brought about the absolute Fall of humanity by sharing the fruit of The Tree of Knowledge with Adam. Sandra M. Gilbert and Susan Gubar, *The Madwoman in the Attic: The Woman Writers and the Nineteenth-century Literary Imagination,* (1979) appear justified in their reading of Milton as 'patriarchal poetry' here. Therefore, for Milton in *PL* it was quintessential that Adam and Eve should not aspire to transcend their naive state, they should remain innocent and ignorant of matters of knowledge, good and evil. Satan had also dared to rebel and suffered awful consequences. Was Milton in the post-revolutionary epoch questioning his earlier positions in support of the revolution and regicide? We will never be able to know exactly what Milton thought but T.S. Eliot made a penetrating comment:

---

[70] Kollontai, Alexandra, *Alexandra Kollontai on Women's Liberation* (London, Bookmarks, 1998), p.48.

The civil war of the seventeenth century, in which Milton is a symbolic figure has never been concluded…Of no other poet is it so difficult to see the poetry simply as poetry, without our theological and political dispositions, conscious and unconscious, inherited and acquired, making an unlawful entry.[71]

It is possible following the current of the primary component of this argument to comprehend Milton's reading of *Genesis* which favours the source 'J' over 'P', his writing on divorce and *PL* generally as a complex series of reflexes of the emergent capitalist and patriarchal society in which he lived. His choice of blank verse and consequent rejection of rhyme was a revolutionary act. The abandonment of his earlier intention to write a patriotic Arthurian epic in favour of an epic in the light of Homer's *Odyssey* and *Iliad*, Virgil's *Aeneid* and Dante's *Divine Comedy* informs us of a profound shift in Milton. He was a man attempting to understand at least three questions: 1) why the revolution had been lost remembering he expected it to be concomitant with the Second Coming and 2) his blindness, surely as profound as Beethoven's deafness, 3) what or who were the English people in the context of the revolutionary and counter-revolutionary events, how did they fit, if at all, into a Divine Cosmology outlined in the *King James Bible*? His answers seemed to be

---

[71] Eliot, T.S. *Milton* (London, Faber & Faber, 1947) p.3.

lacking in consolation for the poet, I would argue, an expulsion from Eden towards introspection:

> but shalt possess
>
> A paradise within thee, happier far.
>
> *PL,* XII L 586 – 587.

Therefore, it could be argued that Milton was abandoning a social project for an inner one and thus possibly bound humanity in manacles.

For Blake in *London* these were 'mind forged manacles':

In every cry of every man,

In every Infant's cry of fear,

In every voice, in every ban,

> The mind-forged manacles I hear[72]

William Blake is expressing the importance of the imagination by attacking what he called the "mind-forged manacles" but does this using an established poetic device called anaphora in which the same word is repeated in every line. He contrasts this in the final line by not employing that device to create a pounding dissonance which reverberates with a full-rhyme 'fear'/'hear.' However, as Raymond Williams suggests there is a social-economic dimension of the power of the capitalist system that at:

---

[72] Blake, William, *The Complete Poems* [ed] Stevenson, W. H. (London, Routledge, 2007), p 161.

the levels of both ideology and actuality, manacle every mind- exploiter and exploited- in an ineluctable organized repression.[73]

However, today humanity is faced with catastrophic climate change which is driven by the logic of capitalism which offers only the abyss and human extinction if not countered by proletarian insurrection[74]. Blake was aware of the dangers of mass industrialization very early as articulated in *Milton: a poem*:

> And did the Countenance Divine,
> Shine forth upon our clouded hills?
> And was Jerusalem builded here,
> Among these dark Satanic Mills?[75]

The 'dark Satanic Mills' are a metaphor for the chaotic and rapid industrialization, which was transforming the English landscape. Blake saw this as Satanic in a similar fashion to Milton's perception of the Restoration. Parallels and disjuncture between these two great poets were to be expected because they were writing within a similar discourse.

However, when we examine the interactions between the two poets Blake's comment is the

---

[73] Williams, Raymond, *The Country and the City* (London, Hogarth Press, 1973) p.148.
[74] Molyneux, John, *Lenin for Today* (London, Bookmarks, 2017) for a cogent argument.
[75] Blake (2007) p, 502.

largest thorn in Milton's side, as here in *Marriage of Heaven and Hell [MHH]:*

> The reason Milton wrote in fetters when he wrote of Angels & God, and at liberty when of Devils & Hell, is because he was a true Poet and of the Devil's party without knowing it.[76]

Blake, self-evidently, predates Shelley's position *In Defence of Poetry* and was the originator of the perspective that Milton's the Devil was a more rounded and sympathetic character than his God. It should be noted that in *MHH* the 'Devil' here, at worst represents 'erroneous thinking' rather than Satan. For Blake in *Songs of Innocence and Experience* the real adversary is the distorting effect of this, like some who would use Milton *PL* as an argument for the repression of 'The soul of sweet delight which should never be defiled.' (Plate 9) and who 'Like caterpillars choose the fairest leaves to lay her eggs on, so the priest lays his curse on the fairest joys.' (Plate.9, 14) with the consequence that:

> Prisons are made out of stones of Law
> , brothels with bricks Of Religion[77]

William Blake *The Poison Tree* which had been originally entitled *Christian Forbearance* in an earlier manuscript:

---

[76] Blake (2007) PL 6, p.113.
[77] Blake (2007) p. 112.

In the morning glad I see
My foe stretched out beneath the tree.[78]
Juxtapose this with a postlapsarian Miltonic Adam:
On the ground
Outstretched he lay, on the cold ground, and oft,
Cursed his creation.
(PL 10:850-1).

The intertextuality is clear, Milton's Father God is understood as tyrannical and cruel.

Blake was like Milton, a revolutionary poet, but he believed Milton must be disencumbered of his belief in God as a reason-driven moralist. As W.H. Stevenson so eloquently encapsulated Blakes beliefs: '(a) that the energies of natural desire, not behaviour to a predetermined code, will lead to the proper way of life… and (b) everyone's 'imagination' is 'the truth' for them. He retained both ideas throughout his life, but they underwent modifications.'[79] Blake might be perceived as a hedonistic solipsist by some, but as he believed that his vision could be generalized to the whole of humankind so one might describe him an early utopian-socialist visionary. As E. P. Thompson pointed out 'It was in the immediate aftermath of the French Revolution that the millennial current… burst open… touched Blake with its breath. Against this background… William Blake seems no longer the cranky untutored genius to those who knew only the genteel culture of the time.'[80]

---

[78] Blake (2007) p. p.210
[79] Blake (2007) p.107.
[80] Thompson, E.P, *The Making of the English Working Class* (London, Pelican, 1968) pp.54-5, 56.

However, Alick West argued 'William Blake was a pioneer. The spirit of his work is not the antagonism of the individual here and society there, but the antagonism within a living unity.'[81] I argue that William Blake understood the essential nature of dialectical thought as he states in *MHH*: 'Without Contraries is no progression.' Ultimately for William Blake there was a dialectical synthesis: 'Are not Religion & Politics the Same Thing? Brotherhood is Religion.' Indeed, Steve Vine argued 'Blake's spiritual-political was, in many ways, an attempt to *reclaim* the popular millenarian tradition that had motivated English revolutionaries in the seventeenth century.'[82] However, neither Eden or its secular equivalent communism can be founded simply on grandiose ideals, like the magnificent dreams of the utopians and poets; it must rest upon a materialist basis. As Engels explained, it is the proletariat itself that can create a historical possibility of the creation of a socialist, classless world:[83]. But and here I unravel the second string of my position because Leon Trotsky *Literature and Revolution* allowed a more complex reading of the dialectical relationship between the socio-economic foundations of

---

[81] West, Alick, *Crisis and Criticism & Literary Essay* (London, Lawrence & Wishart, 1975) pp. 22-23.
[82] Vine, Steve, *William Blake: Writers and their Work* (Northcote, British Council, 2007) p.4.
[83]
https://www.marxists.org/archive/marx/works/1880/soc-utop/

society and that of the literary geniuses created by History. Hence:

But Dante was a genius. He raised the expectations of his epoch to a tremendous artistic height… *The Divine Comedy* as a source of artistic inspiration, this happens not because Dante was a Florentine petty bourgeois of the thirteenth century but, to a considerable extent, in spite of that circumstance.'[84]

We can see in this second augmentation of my argument that our view of John Milton's and William Blake's poetry was enhanced and embellished because like Dante the reader understood they transcended their epoch's fetters of the mundane. This secondary strand compliments rather than obfuscates or dominates the primary.

---

[84] Leon, Trotsky, (2013) p.75

Bibliography.

Primary Sources.

The Bible: Authorized King James version with Apocrypha, (Oxford, Oxford World's Classics, 1997).

Blake, William, *The Complete Poems* [ed] Ostriker, *Alicia* (London, Penguin Classics, 2004).

Blake, William, *The Complete Poems* [ed] Stevenson, W. H. (London, Routledge, 2007),

Carey, John, *The Essential Paradise Lost* (London, Faber & Faber, 2017).

Milton, John, *Areopagitica and Other Writings* (London, (ed) Poole, William (London, Penguin Classics, 2014).

Milton, John, *Paradise Lost* (ed) Fowler, Alastair (London, Routledge, 2006).

Milton, John, *Paradise Lost* [ed] Leonard, John, (London, Penguin Classics, 2003).

Milton, John, *Paradise Lost* (eds) Orgel, Stephen & Goldberg, Jonathan, (Oxford. Oxford University Press, 2008),

Shelley, Percy Bysshe, *The Major Works* (Oxford, Oxford University Press, 2009).

Secondary Sources

Bottrall, M (ed) *Songs of Innocence and Experience: a selection of critical essays* (London, Macmillan Press Limited, 1974.)

Bounds, Philip, *British Communism & the Politics of Literature 1928-1939,* (Pontypool, Merlin Press, 2012)

Broadbent, John, *Paradise Lost: Introduction*, (Cambridge, Cambridge University Press, 2009).

Campbell, Jordan & Corns, Thomas. N, *John Milton: Life, Work, and Thought* (Oxford, Oxford University Press, 2010).

Caudwell, Christopher, *Illusion and Reality* (London, Lawrence & Wishart, 1977).

Danielson, Dennis [ed] *The Cambridge Companion to Milton* (Cambridge, Cambridge University Press, 2013).

Dobranski, Stephen. B (ed) *The Cambridge Introduction to Milton,* (Cambridge, Cambridge University Press, 2012).

Eaves, Morris [ed] *The Cambridge Companion to Blake*, (Cambridge, Cambridge University Press, 2007).

Eliot, T.S. *Milton* (London, Faber & Faber, 1947).

Engels, Frederick *The Northern Star,* 18th December 1847.

Frye, Northrop, *Fearful Symmetry: A Study of William Blake* (U.S.A., Princeton University Press, 1990).

Gilbert, Sandra M and Gubar, Susan: *The Madwoman in the Attic: The Woman Writers and the Nineteenth- century Literary Imagination* (New Haven, Conn, Yale University Press, 1979)

Hill, Christopher, *Milton and the English Revolution* (London, Faber & Faber, 1977).

Hill, Christopher, *The English Bible and the Seventeenth Century Revolution* (London, Allen Lane, The Penguin Press, (1993)

Kean, Margaret (ed) *Paradise Lost: A Sourcebook* (London, Routledge, 2005).

Kollontai, Alexandra, *Alexandra Kollontai on Women's Liberation* (London, Bookmarks, 1998),

Marx, Karl, *Theories of Surplus Value, vol 1* (Moscow, Progress Publishers, 1969),

Marx, Karl & Engels, Frederick, *The Holy Family* (Moscow, Foreign Languages Publishing House, 1956.)

Molyneux, John, *Lenin for Today* (London, Bookmarks, 2017).

Nyquist, Mary The Genesis of Gendered Subjectivity in the Source Traits and in Paradise Lost, (1987) in *Owens, W. R. A815 MA English Course Reader. Part 2 Paradise Lost* (Milton Keynes, The Open University, 2009),

Owens, W. R. *A815 MA English Course Reader. Part 2 Paradise Lost* (Milton Keynes, The Open University, 2009).

Solomon, Maynard, *Marxism and Art* (Detroit, Wayne State University Press, 1979).

Schwartz, Louis, *The Cambridge Companion to Paradise Lost,* (Cambridge, Cambridge University Press, 2014).

Thompson, E.P, *The Making of the English Working Class* (London, Pelican, 1968)

Trotsky, Leon, *Art and Revolution: Writings on Literature, Politics and Culture* (New York, Pathfinder, 2013).

Vine, Steve, *William Blake: Writers and their Work* (Northcote, British Council, 2007).

West, Alick, *Crisis and Criticism & Literary Essays* (London, Lawrence & Wishart, 1975).

Williams, Raymond, *The Country and the City* (London, Hogarth Press, 1973).

Woolf, Virginia, *A Room of One's Own* (London, Penguin Modern Classics, 2000).

Zunder, William, *Paradise Lost: Contemporary Critical Essays* (London, Macmillan Press Limited, 1999).

On Defoe and the colonial encounter.

Daniel Defoe, *Robinson Crusoe*[85] wrote what can be perceived as a paradigm shifting work. It was published in 1719 and immediately went into several editions. The Robinson has become a genre bordering on an archetype. Daniel Defoe had unwittingly created something new. Of course, Cervantes, *Don Quixote*[86], 1605 had already established the long prose-fiction form. But during the 17th century, Portugal and Spain were beginning to wane as Mercantile powers in the face of British colonialism. *Robinson Crusoe* must be understood in the social, economic, indeed historical context that it was written. This was England after it had emerged from a period of social turmoil. However, although the Civil War was passed the bourgeoisie was yet to achieve hegemony in any coherent sense. The contending forces were being reflected in the different literary genre, for example, John Bunyan *A Pilgrims Progress* remarkably written in prison was the literary incarnation of a quintessential Puritan Nonconformity. It was a spiritual allegory. While Daniel Defoe's *novels, Robinson Crusoe* (1719),

---

[85] Daniel Defoe, *Robinson Crusoe*, ed. by Thomas Keymer (Oxford: Oxford University Press, 2008). Hereafter RC1. RC2, RC3.
[86] Miguel De Cervantes Saavedra, *Don Quixote,* ed. by John Rutherford (London, Penguin Classics, 2003).

Moll Fielding[87] (1722), *Roxana*[88] *(1724)* would delineate the lives of society's outsiders. *Robinson Crusoe* was a young man who defied his father's will and the dubious pleasures of middle-class life by running away to sea. Defoe was here, on first examination tuning into the genre of the 'travelogue' which was popular at the time. Particularly the story of Alexander Selkirk *A Cruising Voyage Round the World* (1712)[89]. *Moll Fielding* was born in Newgate Prison and largely lived on her 'wits' and again Defoe used a genre popular with his contemporary audience, the 'Newgate biography', although elaborated on it notably and *Roxane* which within obvious limitations and given the nature of patriarchy at the time could be designated, almost, proto-feminist. It was not published until after Defoe's death. Hence, we can see that these works though were drawing on the sub-genres of the epoch. However, Defoe enhanced and developed them into a new genre, that of 'fictive realism', the phrase employed by Ian Watt in his seminal work *The Rise of the Novel*,[90] to describe the new genre of the novel. They were 'confessional' accounts.

---

[87] Daniel Defoe, *Moll Fielding,* ed. by G.A. Starr and Linda Blee (Oxford: Oxford University Press, 2011).
[88] Daniel Defoe, *Roxana*, ed. by David Blewitt (London, Penguin Books, 1982).
[89] *Rogers, Woodes (1712). A Cruising Voyage Round. beyond the World: First to the South-Sea, Thence to the East-Indies, and Homewards by the Cape of Good Hope. London: A. Bell.*
[90] Ian Watt, *The Rise of the Novel*, (London, The Bodley Head, 2013).

However, I am aware there are other 'readings' of RC1 which I will engage with later, particularly G.A. Starr *Defoe and the spiritual autobiography*[91]. Defoe could be understood as a protean individual who had a varied life in business, journalism, politics but was not a minister of the church. He represented the tendency within the nascent Nonconformist bourgeoisie that would compete and eventually call a truce with Anglicanism and form the new British ruling class. The latter articulated its ideology in a more florid language than that of Nonconformist Protestantism. Nevertheless, England indeed Britain was still an unstable social formulation and Defoe's novels reflected and indeed illuminated this multifaceted ideological uncertainty and competition. This also took place in sermons and religious guidebooks, spiritual autobiographies as well as in the incipient novel. However, almost three hundred years of criticism cannot be avoided. What the critic Pierre Macherey *The Theory of Literary Production*[92],called 'the gaps and silences in a text' compel us to make new interpretations of texts.

The method that I shall employ to examine the issue inherent in the question of the nature of the relationship between narrator and protagonist and

---

[91] G.A. Starr, Defoe and the spiritual autobiography in *Defoe; Critical Impetrations*, ed, by Harold Bloom (Chelsea House Publishers; Library Binding edition Dec. 1991)

[92] Pierre Macherey *The Theory of Literary Production,* (London:1978).

the ironic separation or authorial distance between them emanates from an examination of narratology particularly in Jahn Manfred, *A Guide to the Theory of Narratology*[93], and Claire Colebrook, *Irony: the new critical idiom*[94]. My overarching methodology is derived from Karl Marx and follows thus: "It is not the consciousness of men that determines their existence, but their social existence that determines their consciousness."[95] This fundamental method will be elaborated by examining the work of writers who augmented and developed the Marxist tradition of literary criticism especially three who examined the genre of the novel in detail, George Lukács, Ralph Fox, and Raymond Williams, who developed his own nuanced understanding of Marxism as Cultural Materialism . The writing of Frantz Fanon will be seen to understand Friday in *Black Skin, White Masks*[96] and the nature of the 'settler' in *The Wretched of the Earth*[97]. In regard of the afterlife of *Robinson Crusoe* as a colonial encounter, I shall briefly examine Coetzee *Foe*. All

---

[93] http://www.uni-koeln.de/~ame02/pppn.htm

[94] Claire Colebrook, *Irony: the new critical idiom,* (London: Routledge, *2006) p 179-185.*

[95] Karl Marx, A Contribution to the Critique of Political Economy, Preface. *in Marx & Engels, Selected Works in One Volume* (London, Lawrence & Wishart,1973), p. 180.

[96] Frantz Fanon, *Black Skin, White Masks,* (London: Plato Press, 1986).

[97] Frantz Fanon, *The Wretched of the Earth* (London: Penguin Modern Classics,2001).

these questions are expanded upon and a conclusion achieved.

To arrive at a systematic understanding of the nature of 'Ironic separation' between narrator and protagonist", a prerequisite to the construction of an understanding of the ramifications of the "first contact between Crusoe and Friday" and, therefore, its "implications for the colonial encounter.' I firstly examined Claire Colebrook[98] which understands three main areas of literary irony [from Ancient Greek eirōneía, meaning 'dissimulation, feigned ignorance'. 1) Cosmic Irony, a contrast between the absolute and the relative, the general and the individual, which Hegel called, "general [irony] of the world" or as Claire Coleman argues: 'Cosmic or Tragic irony' is when a community or individual is thwarted by life's events, events which often seem to pass judgement on their life, or seem to be the outcome of fate. 2) dramatic irony when the audience knows more than the characters or 'if a character's speech is undermined by subsequent action' [Ibid] and 3) 'structural irony', this can be understood to be when a fictional hero is a 'first person narrator' and when 'distance' is the extent to which the author draws us into the novel then there are inevitable consequences for this 'first-person narrator' as in RC1. Crusoe tells his story with hindsight which 'Crusoe-on-the-island' cannot have. This is probably close to the concept of "ironic separation." Also, in this context, the question of the 'implied author' is worthy of

---

[98] Colebrook, 2006.

consideration. The 'implied author' cannot, according to Wayne C. Booth, *The Rhetoric of Fiction* [99] who introduced the term of 'implied author' to distinguish the virtual author of the text from the real author. Therefore, we cannot assume in RC1 that there is a direct correlation between the views and beliefs of Danial Defoe and those of Robinson Crusoe. Hence, we can comprehend an additional 'separation' in regard of RC1.Nevertheless, that is not to argue for the 'autonomy' of the text from material conditions because there is a material base for consciousness.

James Joyce brings us face to face with Robinson Crusoe and Friday, indeed Xury, and British colonialism:

> The true symbol of the British conquest is Robinson Crusoe, who, cast away on a desert island, in his pocket a knife and a pipe, becomes an architect, a carpenter, a knife grinder, an astronomer, a baker, a shipwright, a potter, a saddler, a farmer, a tailor, an umbrella-maker, and a clergyman. He is the true prototype of the British colonialist, as Friday (the trusty savage who arrives on an unlucky day) is the symbol of the subject races. The whole Anglo-Saxon spirit is in Crusoe: the manly independence; the unconscious cruelty; the persistence; the slow yet efficient intelligence…
> the practical, well-balanced religiousness; the calculating taciturnity.

---

[99] Wayne C. Booth, *The Rhetoric of Fiction*, (University of Chicago Press, 1983.)

> Whoever rereads this simple, moving book in the light of subsequent history cannot help but fall under its prophetic spell.[100]

The 'footprint in the sand' which foreshadows Crusoe's meeting with Friday has an echo of RC 1, p.53, 'humane Shape had never set Foot upon that Place' and when he does find a single footprint, a stroke of genius from Defoe that Coleridge compared to Shakespeare:

> It happened one Day about Noon going towards my Boat, I was exceedingly surpiz'd with the Print of a Man's naked Foot on the Shore, which was very plain to be seen in the Sand. I stood like one Thunder struck, or if I had seen an Apparition; I listen'd,
> I look'd around me, I could hear nothing, nor see any Thing, I went to a rising Ground to look further I went up the Shore and down the Shore, but it was all one...
>
> RC1, p.130.

This is in itself a beautiful piece of writing and happens with a freedom of style one would expect from the author of a great text. It begins without a trace of anticipation; Crusoe is nonchalant but after what has occurred has been assimilated the pace of the writing is deftly increased by Defoe with short and rapid registers punctuated with commas we are compelled forward with his fear and are left almost breathless. The huge irony as

---

[100] James Joyce, *Lecture on Daniel Defoe*, Università Popolare, Trieste, Italy, March 1912.

pointed out by Pat Rogers *Robinson Crusoe*[101] is that of Crusoe being entrapped on 'the island of despair' in solitude since 1659 in 1674 sees the footprint of a man before he has any palpable evidence of cannibalism but then lives in a state of heightened fear for two years. He does not find the evidence of cannibalism until 1677, has a presentiment in a dream of rescuing a savage from the cannibals and in 1684 he rescues Friday. 1685 being his happiest year on the island as 'Master' of his kingdom complete with Friday and eventually, Friday's father who they freed from cannibals and a Spaniard. Now, this may have fit the narrative of an expansionist British readership in 1719 but the world three hundred years later is a different place. As Heraclitus argued: 'You could not step twice into the same river'. - Plato, *Cratylus*, 402a[102]. History and reality are in motion. and therefore, there are colonial and post-colonial ramifications to Crusoe's perspective, his 'point of view' regarding essentially everyone who is white, male and, maybe, garbed in goatskin.

The first contact with Friday is foreshadowed by a dream in which RC frees two 'savages' and they facilitate his escaping from the island (p.168-9) so he began venturing out of his 'Castle' to 'scout' the shoreline for a year or so, then:

> While I was watching them, I perceived by my Perspective, two miserable Wretches dragg'd from the Boats...and brought

---

[101] Pat Rogers, *Robinson Crusoe* (London: Routledge Revivals, 1979) pp113-116.
[102] https://archive.org/details/dialoguesofplat01plat

out for the Slaughter...In that very Moment this
poor Wretch seeing himself at Liberty...started
away from them, and run with incredible Swiftness
along the sands towards me, I mean towards
that part of the Coast, where my Habitation was.
I was dreadfully frightened...when I perceived him
to run my way...

RC 1, p.170.

RC's response is 'now was the Time to get me a
Servant, and perhaps a Companion, or Assistant;
and that I was call'd by Providence to save this
poor Creature's Life.'RC1, p.171. So, Providence
seemed to be firmly on the side of the British. Yes,
RC had saved his [Friday's] life but it was to firstly
facilitate his escape from the island, and secondly
to provide a 'Servant'. Indeed, the first word Friday
is taught is 'Master.' We will learn that other
Europeans, Spaniards, live peaceably with the
'savages'. So, it became apparent very quickly
there was an ironic separation in this first
encounter, but it is the irony implicit in a Master
race believing that an omniscient Deity can
articulate their narrative and no other. RC comes
to convert Friday, we shall see his own
'conversion experience as ironic. Did Friday have
a choice in the circumstances, he becomes a
better theologian than Crusoe asking why God
allows the devil to exist i.e. a variant on 'the
problem of Evil'. There is also irony in how Crusoe
replicates the master/servant dialectic which is
implicit in Christianity, to that of a master/slave
dialectic between human beings of other origins.
We see this irony of Crusoe with the boy Xury,
whom he escapes slavery with, then converted to

Christianity only to 'sell' him. The ironies between how RC behaves and the consequences he later draws from his behaviour are marked. Coetzee argued

> *Robinson Crusoe* is unabashed propaganda for the establishment of new British colonies. As for the native peoples of the Americas and the obstacle they represent, all one need say is that Defoe chooses to represent them as cannibals. The treatment Crusoe metes out to them is accordingly, savage.[103]

For the modern reader acquainted with Frantz Fanon, who was a French Martiniquian, both the ideas of self-subjection of a colonial people and their path to emancipation becomes clearer. In *Black Skin, White Masks*[104] he argued that white racism was a complex problem having understood that many of his countrymen had negrophilic tendencies. He explained this by arguing that they had internalized white stereotypes and rejected their own 'blackness' and demonized other Black people, Black Africans. Hence one can see a black person ashamed of their colour wearing a white mask. Therefore, Frantz Fanon argued here that white-blacks must somehow be emancipated from the complex which alienated them from their Black sisters and brothers and the whites from their feelings of superiority and stereotyping of

---

[103] Coetzee, J.M. *stranger shores essays 1956-1999* (London, Vintage, 2002), p 24.
[104] Fanon (1986).

black people. We can perceive Friday here as a Black man who has put on a white mask. In both this regard and that of RC generally, Frantz Fanon is clear in *The Wretched of the Earth:*

The settler makes history and is conscious of making it. And because he constantly refers to the history of his mother country, he clearly indicates that he himself is the extension of that mother-country. Thus, the history which he writes is not the history of the country which he plunders but the history of his own nation in regard to all that she skims off, all that sheviolates and starves.[105]

Virginia Woolf [106], a contemporary of James Joyce, had argued in her bi-centennial assessment that RC1 was had been absorbed into consciousness as an archetype. However, more interesting for the purposes of my analysis she returned to the subject in *The Common Reader* Volume 2. 'He is incapable of enthusiasm. He has a natural slight distaste for the sublimities of Nature. He suspects even Providence of exaggeration.' [107] Albert Camus was to write of the art of fiction: 'fiction is the lie through which we tell the truth.' Certainly, this was true in the novel in the 20th century but Defoe wrote in RC3 (1720): 'This supplying a story by the invention is certainly

---

[105] Fanon, 2001, p.40.
[106] Virginia Woolf, *The Common Reader, vol. 1* (London: Vintage, 2003).
[107]

https://ebooks.adelaide.edu.au/w/woolf/virginia/w91c2/chapter4.html

a scandalous crime. It is a sort of lying that makes a great hole in the heart, in which a habit of lying enters in.' Here we can observe the Nonconformist Puritan suspicion of both the theatre and prose-fiction. Thus, there is most definitely 'ironic separation at the very heart of Defoe's multi-volume project. Crusoe-the-protagonist-on-the-island and Crusoe-the-narrator-of-RC1 and Crusoe-the – narrative voice-of-RC3. There is no doubt that RC3 clenches the point for an inherent ironic separation as it is a quasi-mystical commentary. The ironic gap between: 'I was born in the Year 1632, in the City of York, of a good family.' RC1, p.1 to RC3 p.365: 'The Fable is always made for the Moral, not the Moral for the Fable.' Defoe is asking his reader to read RC as a parable here. However, two paragraphs later he is warning his reader:

> Robinson Crusoe, being at this time in perfect and sound mind and memory, thanks be to God therefor, do hereby declare their objection is an invention scandalous in design, and false in fact; and do affirm that the story, though allegorical, is also historical.
>
> RC3, p 365.

G.A. Starr[108] is interesting and attempts to shed light on RC1 and religiosity. However, the premise for Starr's contribution revolves around Crusoe's "conversion experience" RC1, pp.80-83. The point I would like to make in that regard is that it is a rather Worldly "conversion experience" when RC sees an avenging angel with a spear

---

[108] In Bloom (1991).

who threatens him. He was not only ill and this is my point, he had altered his state of consciousness with copious amounts of alcohol 'a pint of rum' mixed with water and strong tobacco:

> I found a cure both for Soul and Body. I open'd the Chest, and found what I was looking for, viz. the Tobacco, and the few Books, I had sav'd, lay there too, I took out one of the Bibles which I mention'd before...and brought both that and the Tobacco with me to the table. the Tobacco at first almost stupefied my brain being green and strong...then I took some rum...In the interval of this, I took up the Bible and began to read.
>
> RC1, p. 80.

So, RC upon reflection:

> My Condition began now to be, tho' miserable as to my Way of living, yet much easier to my Mind; my Thoughts being directed by a constant reading of Scripture, and praying to God...
>
> RC1, p.83.

Any reader may see a little irony here and the modern reader most certainly perceives Crusoe as desperate, ill and maybe intoxicated when he opens the Bible. Starr (1965) does provide contemporary data as to physical illness being linked to 'conversion experiences' but not, I think with the assistance of a 'pint of rum' and 'strong tobacco.'

For George Lukács[109], arguing from a classical Marxist perspective the novel was a product of capitalism and therefore embodied man in his social nexus. It was thus a Realist genre and we are aware of the nature of verisimilitude in RC1 and RC2. Indeed, this whole tradition of literary critics perceived the novel to be a great product of a revolutionary class, the bourgeoisie especially until the revolutions of 1848 when they understood that social class had become reactionary and a fetter on Humanity's development. Ralph Fox described 'the novel as the great gift to humanity from the bourgeoisie.' [110] Indeed, for theoreticians of this persuasion the social production of human beings, our interaction with the environment and the dialectic between humanity and Nature which Marx calls 'labour' whether physical or intellectual is what the young Marx maintained provided humanity with its "species-being", its essence [see Marx, *Philosophical and Economic Manuscripts of 1844*]. Here Marx illustrates the process under the circumstances of 'commodity production' and its distortion:

The worker becomes all the poorer the more wealth he produces, the more his production increases in power and size. The worker becomes an ever-cheaper commodity the more commodities he creates.
The devaluation of the world of men is in direct proportion to the increasing value of the

---

[109] George Lukács, *The Historical Novel* (London: Merlin Press, 1965.)

[110] Ralph Fox, *The Novel and the People* (London: Lawrence & Wishart, 1979), p 53.

world of things. Labour produces not only commodities; it produces itself and the worker as a commodity – and this at the same rate at which it produces commodities in general.

This fact expresses merely that the object which labour produces – labour's product – confronts it as something alien, as a power independent of the producer. The product of labour is labour which has been embodied in an object, which has become material: it is the bjectification of labour. Labour's realization is its objectification. Under hese economic conditions this realization of labour appears as loss of realization for the worker's objectification as loss of the object and bondage to it; appropriation as estrangement, as alienation [111]

It is the 'estrangement' of labour from its object and the artificial 'division of labour' between manual and mental labour that is pertinent here and which I shall explore further in the analysis of the 'island narrative' in RC1 which will be comprehended as, a laboratory, almost approximating *tableau rasa* in the sense that Defoe's contemporary philosophers, the British Empiricists, would have understood.

RC is cast into a circumstance on the island where the capitalist relations of production are, self-evidently, not dominant. We can see a 17th century Englishman having to start from scratch.

---

[111] Marx, K, *Philosophical and Economic Manuscripts of 1844*, (Moscow: Progress Publishers, 1967) p 66

He has salvaged some tools and munitions from the wrecked ship. But, he is not *tableau rasa* and merely reproduces the relations of society he originated from. British colonialism was not in the blood but as I had quoted previously from Marx 'social being determines consciousness.' There was not a 'necessity' for RC to reproduce the relationships and power hierarchies of the metropolitan country on his island, but he did without any intended irony. Was there an alternative. Marx's *Capital* provides one:

> Let us picture to ourselves, by way of change, a community of free individuals, carrying out their work with the means of production in common...All the characteristics of Robinson's labour are here repeated, but with the difference that they are social, instead of an individual. Everything produced by him was exclusively the result of his own personal labour, and simply an object of use by himself. The total product of our community is a social product. [112]

So, it is not labour that is the problem, but how it is organized and RC1 having created a microcosm allowed us to think creatively about this question and envisage potential solutions such as the social ownership of 'the means of production.'

Thus, 'commodity-production' and the division of labour i.e., capitalism was finding its earliest development in Britain with its concomitant ideology of individualism. In this epoch, that of RC1, there was social uncertainty and competition

---

[112] Marx, K *Capital, vol 1* (London, Pelican Marx Library, 1976) p 169

in early capitalism which Raymond Williams[113] aptly described as a 'crisis of values.'. This was a huge structural change in England, Williams argued: 'The transition from feudal and immediate post-feudal arrangements to this developing agrarian capitalism is of course immensely complex. But its social implications are clear enough...In this development, an ideology of self-improvement...became significant.' Defoe, argues Raymond Williams (ibid, pp 88-89), with some merit, abstracted the crisis and shock of the coming together of pastoral and industrial forces at the turn of the century when he began writing novels that he would project: 'the abstracted spirit of improvement and simple economic advantage – as most noteworthy in Robinson Crusoe – and created a fictional world of isolated individuals to whom other people are basically transitory and functional.' (ibid) We can understand this because the young Crusoe rejected his father's entreaties to remain in: 'the middle state, or what might be called the upper Station of Low life, which he had found by long experience was the best in the World.' (RC1 p.2). Society was experiencing a maelstrom, what Williams described as the 'Pastoral and the Anti-Pastoral, the country and the city' and, of course consequently, the emergence of the last two great contending classes of History, the bourgeoisie, and the proletariat.

---

[113] Raymond Williams, *The Country and the City* (London: Vintage, 2016) p.86

I want to return to the consequence of the colonial encounter: Edward Said argued:

> I am not trying to say that the novel or the culture in the broad sense – 'caused imperialism, but that the novel as a cultural artifice of bourgeois society, and imperialism are unthinkable without the other.[114]

Coetzee, *Foe, 1986,* [115] is an attempt at 'writing back' to RC1. In its method in challenges the Realism of the master narrative by introducing a woman, Susan Barton who is modelled on a character in *Roxana*. However, although this feminist dimension is significant because Susan Barton wants Foe to write her island narrative into a popular genre which has irony. However, I am interested here in the post-colonial; 'writing back' or indeed lack of it. Friday is in the care of Susan as he is mute, possibly because his tongue has been mutilated or there is an inference it could be psychological. Dominic Head[116] argues he may be castrated as well. Friday's silence sets up what Dominic Head called a 'double-bind' situation in the novel because Coetzee as the author is a white man commenting on Black oppression and Susan tries to teach Friday to speak again. They represent the position of white liberals in post-

---

[114] Edward Said, *Culture and Imperialism, (London, Vintage, 1993) p.84.*
[115] Coetzee, *Foe,* (Penguin Books, London 1986).
[116] Dominic Head, *The Cambridge Introduction to Coetzee*, (Cambridge, Cambridge University Press, 2009) pp, 63-65

colonial situations, essentially marginalized. Friday's silence can only be perceived as a metaphor for a deafening roar as he is an emblem of the people Frantz Fanon *The Wretched of the Earth* described in the colonial situation, 'The well-being and progress of Europe have been built up with the sweat and dead bodies of Negros'. His solution was the National Liberation struggles of brown, black and yellow people. This was Frantz Fanon's position during the Algerian War of Independence in 1961:

> At the level of the individual, violence is a cleansing power. It frees the individual from his inferiority complex and from his despair and inaction…Even if the armed struggle has been symbolic…the people have the time to see that the liberation has been the business of each and all and that the leader has no special merit[117].

Fanon's words haunt us 300 years after *Robinson Crusoe* was published with a resonance which leaves the European as "Thunder struck" as Robinson Crusoe when he discovered that solitary footprint in the sand. A remorseless dialectic as Marx argued: 'A nation which enslaves another can never itself be free.'[118] We see the imperialist as a dissembler.

---

[117] Frantz Fanon 2001, p.74.
[118] https://www.marxists.org/archive/marx/works/1870

Bibliography.

Primary Sources.

Miguel De Cervantes, *Don Quixote,* ed. by John Rutherford (London, Penguin Classics, 2003).

Defoe, D, *Moll Fielding,* ed. by G.A. Starr and Linda Blee (Oxford: Oxford University Press, 2011).

Defoe, D, *Robinson Crusoe*, ed. by Thomas Keymer (Oxford: Oxford University Press, 2008).

Defoe, D, *The Complete Life of Robinson Crusoe*, ed, by S. M. Rogers (U.S.A.).

Defoe, D, *Roxana*, ed. by David Blewitt (London, Penguin Books, 1982).

Rogers, Woods. A Cruising Voyage Roed. by und the World: First to the South-Sea, Thence to the East-Indies, and Homewards by the Cape of Good Hope. (London: A. Bell, 1712).

Secondary Sources.

Ashcroft, B, Griffins, G and Tiffin, H eds. *Postcolonial Studies: The Key Concepts,* Third Edition (London: Routledge, 2013).

Baines, P *Danial Defoe: Robinson Crusoe/Moll Flanders, A reader's guide to essential criticism* (London: Palgrave MacMillan).

Bounds. P, *British Communism & the Politics of Literature 1928-1939*, (Pontypool: Merlin Press, 2012).

Coetzee, J.M. *Foe,* (Penguin Books, London 1986).

Coetzee, J.M. *stranger shores essays 1956-1999* (London, Vintage, 2002)

Fanon, F, *Black Skin, White Masks,* (London: Plato Press, 1986).

Fanon, F, *The Wretched of the Earth* (London: Penguin Modern Classics, 2001).

Fox, R, *The Novel and the People (London: Lawrence & Wishart, 1979),*

Head, D, *The Cambridge Introduction to Coetzee,* (Cambridge, Cambridge University Press, 2009).

Hammond, P, *A Defoe Companion* (London: McMillian Press,1993).

Joyce, J, *Lecture on Daniel Defoe*, Università Popolare, Trieste, Italy, March 1912.

Kettle, A, *Literature, and Liberation: Selected Essays* ed. by Graham Martin and W. R. Jones (Manchester: Manchester University Press1988).

Kettle, A, *An Introduction to the English Novel vol 1*, (London: Hutchinson & Co, 1977).

Lukács, G, *The Historical Novel* (London: Merlin Press, 1965).

Macherey, P, *The Theory of Literary Production,* (London:1978).

Mackay, M, *The Cambridge Introduction to the Novel* (Cambridge: Cambridge University Press, 2011).

Marx, K, A Contribution to the Critique of Political Economy, Preface. *in Marx & Engels, Selected Works in One Volume* (London, Lawrence & Wishart,1973).

Marx. K, *Capital, vol 1 (*London, Pelican Marx Library, 1976),

Marx, K, *Philosophical and Economic Manuscripts of 1844*, (Moscow: Progress Publishers, 1967).

Rogers, P, ed. *Defoe The Critical Heritage* (London: Routledge & Kegan Paul Ltd, 1972).

Rogers, *P, Robinson Crusoe*, (Routledge Revivals, 1979).

Said, E, *Culture and Imperialism, (London, Vintage, 1993).*

G. A. Starr, Defoe and the spiritual autobiography in *Defoe; Critical Interpretations.* ed, by Harold Bloom (Chelsea House Publishers; Library Binding edition Dec. 1991).

Watt, I *The Rise of the Novel* (London, The Bodley Head, 2015).

Williams, R, *The Country and the City* (London: Hogarth Press,1993).

Woolf, V, *The Common Reader, vol 1* (London: Vintage, 2003).

What is literature?

Roman Jacobson maintained:

'Literature is organized violence committed on everyday language.'

Jacobson, Roman in Eagleton, Terry *Marxism and Literature*, (1976).

The question 'what is literature?' is a literary device in that it is a rhetorical question, it elicits an answer. I shall argue or sketch many well-established replies and allow you to reach your own conclusions. Literature and poetry can be differentiated from other writing or speech by having the quality of 'literariness'. This term was first employed by the Russian Formalist Critic Roman Jacobson in 1919 when he declared:

The subject of literary scholarship is not literature in its totality, but literariness, that is, that which makes a given work of literature.

Jacobson, Roman [1919] in Victor Erich (1981) p, 171, *Russian Formalism*; History, Doctrine, Yale University Press.

So, for the Russian Formalists literature was not the incarnation of: The best that has been thought and said in the world.

Arnold, Mathew ([1869] (1971) *Culture and Anarchy*, p,6. Cambridge University Press.

Secular religion as Mathew Arnold argued, would save Western capitalist civilization from both the creeping philistinism of the rising bourgeoisie and the degeneration of the masses and that this may bring about social disorder. Arnold was hoping to make cultural glue, a kind of cultural opium of the people. It would by implication require a transcendental quality inherent in an ether of eternal 'Ideas'. The Canon of bourgeois texts is to be read with the guiding hand of a bourgeois curriculum e.g. 'The Newbolt Report'.

However, there was disagreement between the Russian Formalists who deviated from the concept held by most other Marxists that literature was simply a reflection in the ideological superstructure of the material base of any given socio-economic epoch, 'in the last instant.' The views of the Formalists were unorthodox although most remained close to the ideas of the Bolshevik revolution and their ideas around them which went out of favour with the rise of the Stalinist counter-revolution. Leon Trotsky learning from and leaning towards the Russian Formalists claimed artistic creation is:

A deflection, a changing and transformation of reality, in accordance with the laws of art.

Trotsky, Leon (1924) Literature and Revolution in Eagleton, Terry Marxism and Literary Criticism (2002), p. 46 Routledge.

The key to understanding the ideas of the Formalists lies in this concept of 'literariness'. They argued that in everyday language and literature we develop habits or are 'automatized' by the routine of everyday life. We simply may not notice literature when we are reading it because of it does not possess this quality of 'literariness'. What gives something, a material text, this quality? It is 'defamiliarization' argued Victor Shklovsky in an important text, Poetry as Technique (1917) and this is central to the ripening of the human experience:

'Art exists that one may recover the sensation of life... The purpose of art is to impart the sensation of things as they are perceived not as they are known.'

Shklovsky, Victor (1917) Poetry as Technique in Hans Bertens (2008) Literary Theory. p 25 Routledge.

It serves a similar purpose to that which the English poet Shelley had claimed for poetry in A Defence of Poetry (1821):

Poetry lifts the veil from the hidden beauty of the world and makes familiar objects be as they were not familiar'   Shelley (1821) In Defence of Poetry

This of course poses the question of how a material text transmutes from a piece of everyday language or 'autotomised' experience in a piece of 'literature' this is what made this small group so radical. For there were suggesting that it lies in the formulaic devices within a text, rhythm, metaphor, image etc. That in turn lead to them being labelled in a derogatory manner 'Formalists', but it is also what underpins their perspective to a firm commitment to the material text. They tended towards understanding the materiality of the text as its primary importance and the literary devices which allowed this text to attain literariness which is consistent with a Materialist analysis derived from Marx and following Marxism the Russian Formalists comprehended 'texts' as being significant in the context of the social and economic period they were written in. However, they were clearly not 'Orthodox' literary Marxist scholars in the manner of Georg Lukács. Indeed, it is illuminating to examine the debate between Victor Shklovsky and Georg Lukács to inform the differences to the Formalist and this more 'orthodox' Marxist approach to literature. The orthodox approach to art is encapsulated by Plekhanov, the 'father of Russian Marxism':

As an adherent of the materialist conception of the world, I would say that the first task of the art critic is to translate the ideas of a work of art from the language of art into the the language of sociology, to establish what might be called the sociological equivalent of a given literary phenomenon.

See Plekhanov, G.V. (1955) Kunst and Literatur, Berlin And again by Lukács when he argues artistic concentration:

Is the maximum intensification in content of the social? and human essence of a given situation. Lukács, G (1978) Writer and Critic, London.

It is possible to perceive how the Formalists were concerned with the 'defamiliarization' or 'strangeness' of the individual literary text, what made it different and unique what they called its '' literariness'; but literalness was critical for Lukács. For him the average person in the historical

Realist novel was of the most significant as they 'reflected' authentic social relations and in all its contradictions. His criticism of Shklovsky and of the Formalists generally was scathing, for them:

The average character is nothing but an embodiment of uninspiring pedestrianism. Tihanov, G (2000) Victor Shklovsky and George Lukács in the 1930's. University College London.

So, in conclusion to the question 'what is literature?' 1) is it as Mathew Arnold, argued the quintessence of the 'best of humanity' transmogrified into a secular religion, 2) a special kind of writing which has the effect of 'defamiliarization' and therefore gives a text its literariness and allows the reader to see reality in a new light as the Russian Formalists maintained or 3) Georg Lukács' argument that it should represent everyday life and show its contradictions. I will leave the last words to Lenin:

One cannot life in society and be free of society. The freedom of the bourgeois writer is simply masked dependence on money.

We socialists expose this hypocrisy and rip off false labels, not to arrive at a non-class literature (that will only be possible in a socialist non-class society) ...It will then be a free literature, become, the idea of socialism and sympathy with working people and not greed or careerism. 'Down with literary supermen! Literature must become part of the common cause of the proletariat, "cog and screw" of a gradualist mechanism set in motion by the entire vanguard of the the entire working class.'

Lenin. V. I. (1905) Party Organization and Party Literature, pp. 2-5. Moscow

On creativity, exorcism and recovery.

Creativity is a means of exorcising the ghosts that haunt your soul, torment your mind. The pen can do more than any priest or shaman.

'Many of the most sincere and gifted artists and writers in this capitalist world are conscious of a loss of reality.'

- Ernst Fischer: 'The Necessity of Art'.

Some theorists of language, such as the 'Russian Formalists' have argued that this 'loss of reality' is a positive aspect to writing and the processes of language generally. The 'Formalists' existed before the revolution of October 1917 in Russia and thrived in the creativity of the post-revolutionary period of the 1920's, only to be crushed by the counter-revolutionary Stalinists during the 1930's. They moved attention away from the symbolist interpretation of literature to a more material approach to the text. What is of interest to us about them is the 'concept' of the 'defamiliarizing effect' or what they called 'making strange'. The first step of their argument is that literature is condensed by Jan Mukarosky:

'in the maximum of the foregrounding of the utterance, that is bring the act of expression to the foreground, into prominence for the reader.'

- Mukarosky.

The concept of foregrounding therefore is to put the 'linguistic medium' i.e. literature at the front of our perceptions. Victor Shklovsky argues this creates estrangement or a defamiliarizing effect, by disrupting the everyday uses of language literature 'makes strange' the world of everyday life a and renews the readers lost capacity for a new experience; essentially literature disrupts the 'mundane' which is part of our experience of alienation under capitalism. Therefore, it is possible to argue that a 'loss of reality' or even the process of 'making strange' can be understood as positive elements in writing.

Having established the idiosyncratic nature of 'authentic' writing I will now construct a model of consciousness and language as formed by Marx and Engels which will then be developed by the philosophy of language created by Valentin Voroshilov in the late 1920's. Then this model will be applied to the journey taken by Jean-Paul Sartre from his first novel of 1938: 'Nausea' which is a work of existential dread and horror which expresses the essence of Sartre's existentialism to his crowning philosophical text: 'Critique of Dialectical Reason' which offers a path to freedom through 'praxis' from the existential anguish of his early novel.

Firstly, then how did Marx and Engels conceptualize and therefore understand the categories of and the relationship between consciousness and language? The response is multi-dimensional a) Marx to quote Terry Eagleton:

'Turned the whole history of philosophy of humanity on its head, revolutionized it with the statement: 'my method is movement upwards from the abstract to the concrete.'

- Eagleton.

This is the foundation for the overarching thesis I present here i.e. Historical and Dialectical Materialism. For Marx and Engels, we live in a material world. b) The material source of consciousness is material:

'Thought and consciousness are products of the human brain.'

- Engels.

This may seem obvious, but for many people the source of awareness is not the brain but 'The Idea' (Hegel), a 'First Cause' (Aristotle) or a 'Supreme Being' (Thomas Aquinas). So, what is the nature of this 'consciousness' described by Engels?

First came labour; after it, and then side by side with it, articulate speech.'

- Engels.

This process is social and the result of people not only interacting with their environment but each other:

'in order to produce they enter definite connections and relations with one another, and within these social connections and relations does their activity take place.'

- Marx.

Therefore, labour and language are social in nature. This position is developed further:

'First labour, then articulate speech were the two main stimuli under the influence of which the brain of the ape gradually changed into the human brain. The development of labour brought the members of the community more closely together...these relations gave rise to the need for primitive man to speak and communicate with each other.'

-
Schneierson.

Here, therefore, is the fundamental model on which this thesis is constructed upon. Now I will look at two models of language in the light of the model constructed above. First, Ferdinand de Saussure in his 'Course of General Linguistics' (1913) created a theory which would influence all following study of language. It consisted of a) There exists a pre-established or ahistorical structure of language before its realization as writing and speech.

b) It consisted of chains of 'signs'. Each 'sign' is made up of 1) Signifier which is the sound or written image of 2) the Signified or meaning/concept. e.g. in English the signifier 't r e' is related to the signified Tree and therefore creates the word TREE. But this is random because in other languages the signified tree would have a different signifier...

because for Saussure this structure is detached from socio-history it is profoundly opposed to Marxism, but a Russian Marxist linguist named Valentin Voroshilov took it up in a study called 'Marxism and the Study of Language' (1929). He accepted the concept of the 'sign':

'The entire reality of a word is absorbed in being a 'sign'.

- Voroshilov.

However, ideology which here means both ideas and 'false consciousness' (Marx) is transmitted through language:

'everything ideological possesses semiotic (sign) value'.

- ibid.

So, for Voroshilov the false dichotomy between the material base and ideological superstructure of classical Marxism is resolved through language or 'signs'. However, he recognizes the limitations of the 'sign'

'Signs only arise...they become material only socially, they comprise a group and only then do they take (real) shape.'

-ibid.

But it is when 'sign' or words become what Saussure had called 'parole' or 'utterances' that they become significant i.e. both material and socially interactive. Language is as Engels had argued a defining human characteristic. Voroshilov enhances this position:

'In point of fact, the word is a two-sided act. It is determined equally by whose word it is and for whom it is meant.'

The 'word' therefore introduces not monologue but dialogue...we communicate with others, he concludes:

'A word is the product of the reciprocal relationship between speaker and listener. Each word the 'one in relation to the other"

- ibid.

I would now like to apply this theoretical construct to the journey taken by Jean-Paul Sartre from the existentialist 'dread' of his novel 'Nausea' (1938) to the concept of 'praxis' as a path to freedom in 'Critique of Dialectical Reason' (1960). A path through human creativity as social rather than merely individual which be the solution to 'absurdity' characterized as mental health issues. The central character in 'Nausea' says;

'The nausea has not left me, I think it will be some time before it does...it is no longer an illness or passing fit: it is I.'

- Sartre (1938).

The words nausea or sickness appear in two other of Sartre's works; 1) 'The Psychology of the Imagination' (1940) 'are conscious of a nauseating sickness.' and 2) in his first major philosophical work 'Being and Nothingness' (1943) 'dullness...feeling of sickness.' Why? Sartre defines three modes of being a) 'Being-in- itself' this are objects which simply exist like a tree, b) 'Being-for-itself' this is humanity, because we have no pre-determined essence, there is no 'First Cause', for Sartre, we make ourselves, we create ourselves. It is the absurd contrast between these two forms of being which is one cause for Nausea, c) 'Being-for-Others', here Sartre says we only become aware of our 'being' when in the 'gaze' of another, when someone 'looks' at you. Thus:

'I find myself in a state of instability in relation to the Other.'

- Sartre (1943).

This is where Sartre's infamous phrase 'Hell is other people' is derived from. Any belief in a system of ideas or faith was, according to Sartre currently, 'bad faith'. But Sartre discovered the analytical tools provided by Marx and Engels and renewed them to explain and transcend this existential dread or 'Nausea' in 'Critique of Dialectical Reason': 1) he embraced Marx's concept of conscious human activity as the dynamic of History, once this was established he had to explain his early position of 'Nausea', 2) to achieve this Sartre created the idea of the 'Practico-inert' which is when humans are active but not social like atoms whirling around in a system and 3) he provided the solution of 'praxis' or 'depasssement' (going beyond the existing situation). This is a refinement of Marx's concept of 'species-being' which was, he said, the essence of humans i.e. to act interact with the world and each other. For Sartre 'praxis' and 'activity' are at the heart of the solution. This 'praxis' is genuine social activity created and made two-way by language:

'We set off from the immediate, the individual fulfilling him/herself to the totality of bonds with others...absolute concrete people.'

- Sartre (1960).

The social is creative, and the creative is social, they are only divided in a social system which has what Marx called the 'division of labour' between mental and manual labour and ultimately between those who are compelled to sell 'social labour', which is their creativity, and to those who buy and profit from it. But the only way to prevent the commoditization of art is to abolish commodity capitalism; one is dependent on the other. But maintaining an active dialogue between artists and writers is a key step in breaking the chains of mental ill health and aiding recovery. Pick up you pen and write, and the chains of illness will dissolve.

The Situationist International: then and now.

'The spectacle is the moment when the commodity has achieved the total occupation of social life.'

- Guy Debord: 'The Society of the Spectacle.'

Who were the Situationist International (S.I.), what did they believe and how influential have their ideas been since their dissolution in 1972? These questions can be answered by examining:1) the avant-garde movements in art and literature that first inspired the S.I., 2) the founding of the S.I. in 1957 and the ideas that they fused at that moment, 3) the split in 1962 and the creation of the Second S.I., 4) the rise of Guy Debord and the revolutionary upheavals in Paris in 1968, 5) the impact of Situationist ideas in the politico-cultural scene in the UK during the 1970's and 6) the positions of individual Situationists today.

Firstly, one of the avant-garde groups which influenced the Situationists was the Dadaists. They had complex sources for their radical art critiques which they vigorously applied to both their art and lives. Dada embraced the 'new' in his 1918 manifesto:

'I am writing a manifesto and there's nothing I want, and yet I'm saying certain things, and in I am against manifestos, as I am against principles…Liberty DADA, DADA; the roar of contorted pains, the interweaving of contraries and of all contradictions, freaks and irrelevances LIFE.'

And Arthur Rimbaud who had said:

(the poet should) become a seer by a long, prodigious and rational disordering of all his senses (embracing all forms) of love, of suffering, of madness.'

- Arthur Rimbaud.

However, the avant-garde was inevitably linked to the oppressed and Dada's art had flourished in the working-class movement. Situationist writer Mustapha Khayati would later argue that:

'Dada had a chance for realization with the Spartacus's, with the revolutionary practice of the German proletariat, (their failure) made the failure of Dada inevitable.'

The S.I. formed itself at a small village in Italy on July 28th, 1957. Their intention was to reactivate radical art movements like Dada and Surrealism. However they came to the conclusion that Dada was the end of art in the West and that a new form of creativity was necessary:

'The modern artist does not paint but creates directly... Life and art are One.'

- Tristan Tzara.

Emboldened the S.I. produced a journal called 'Internationale Situationist' in 1958 which contained an important insight into the direction the S.I. would move:

'A new form of mental illness has swept the planet: banalisation. Everyone is hypnotized, by work and comfort: by the...washing machine. The liberation of man from material cares (has) become a life-destroying obsession.'

- Gilles Ivain. I.S. 1, 1958.

A key moment in the development of the S.I. came in 1962 when a split occurred and a Second S.I. created which was interested in what could be called pure art. The 'French Section' and its main theoretician Guy Debord became the dominant force and he began to apply the ideas of the S.I. to Marx's theory of alienation. Marx had said a worker under capitalism only:

'Feels himself outside his work, and in his work feels outside himself. He feels at home when he is not working, and when he is working does not feel at home.'

- Karl Marx.

Alienated from their own labour (for Marx labour is the 'species being' of humanity) these relations of alienation are reproduced throughout capitalism. Debord in his 1968 book 'The Society of the Spectacle' had refined these ideas into the concept of the 'spectacle':

1. 'The entire life of societies in which modern production heralds itself as an accumulation of spectacles.'

2. 'The spectacle is not an aggregate of images but a social relation among people, mediated by images.'

3. 'The spectacle is capital accumulated to such a degree it becomes an image.'

Debord quoted a letter to Marx from Ruge (1844) towards the conclusion: 'Shall we live long enough to see a social revolution.'

In May 1968 French students rioted, the workers occupied factories and a huge General Strike began, the S.I. was at a pinnacle. After the defeat of the revolution the S.I. collapsed into endless theoretical debate and personal animosity dissolving itself in 1972. However the ideas of the S.I. were sown in the underground scene of the UK and influenced groups like the 'Angry Brigade' who spoke with a fist and the 'Sex Pistols' who howled with music.

An unorthodox Situationist UK terrorist group called the 'Angry Brigade' carried out activities 1969-1973. Most of their operations were against property, but this did not prevent the state from giving them very long prison sentences. However they carried out a number of symbolic attacks:1) Minister of Employment, Richard Carr, had his house bombed during the strikes against the Industrial Relations Act and 2) An attack on Miss World contest in 1970 showed solidarity with the Women's Movement. The Brigade hoped that the spontaneity of the 'autonomous working class' would be triggered and the 'spectacle' broken. However the S.I. had been critical of terrorist tactics in 1969:

'From the strategical perspective of social struggles it must first be said we should never play with terrorism.'

- Internationale Situationiste 1969.

The Angry Brigade was imprisoned in 1973, some for 30 years.

Malcolm McLaren had been acquainted with the pro-Situationist group 'King Mob' in the early 1970's and he was therefore aware of Situationist texts. Later he set up a shop called 'Sex' which became a 'hang-out' for those interested in cultural rebellion; he formed from the circle that grew around him there the punk-rock band 'The Sex Pistols.'

'a tide of nihilistic refusal of the spectacle was initiated.'

- Sadie Plant.

A pamphlet called 'The End of Music' produced in 1978 was circulated around the scene; it described 'punk' as a movement with:

'no desire to negate music…merely to make it free.'

But after a brief blooming of creativity, individualism and some solidarity the 'punk' movement was assimilated back into the 'spectacle'. But McLaren had before that injected fresh life into the Situationist critique for a new generation. Punk had claimed as DADA did that anybody could be a poet and that art was radical. Punk, a major working-class movement, had drowned in commercialism and hedonism. The decline of Sid Vicious into heroin addiction and the death of both Sid and his partner Nancy were like bells toiling, ringing out the end of punk. However we can see how the fundamental concepts of the S.I. continued and were metamorphosed in the UK.

What are the Situationists saying now? One of the leading French intellectuals from previous struggles, Raoul Vaneigem, is tuning into a tendency within Situationist thought that can be traced back to the first issue of 'Internationale Situationiste' in 1958 (see above). He argued in 2000 that:

1. 'Time spent working is time lost…time which you would otherwise be free to spend however one wished.'

2. 'In the commodity system the aim of obligatory work is to churn out commodities…Commodities have no purpose other than to sustain the profits and power of the ruling class.'

3. 'By accumulating and replacing commodities with your obligatory work you are merely boosting the power of the bosses.'

Therefore, the argument is 'don't do obligatory work' as a method of breaking the 'spectacle'. This is similar to the first recorded piece of Situationist graffiti which was on the 'Left Bank' in Paris in 1957; it reads 'never work.'

A final solution to the hegemony of the bourgeoisie can only lie in, as Marx argued, an active class-conscious proletariat. S.I. had said correctly in 1963:

'We don't claim to be developing a new revolutionary programme all by ourselves.'

On the revolutionary poetry of Bertolt Brecht.

' The poet has watched the people's mouth.' - Bertolt Brecht.

Bertolt Brecht is probably best known for his experimental plays and the dramatic theory he developed around them. But he was also one of the most important poets of the 20th century and arguably the most significant Marxist poet of this epoch, he wrote 1,500 poems. But he also entered into debates over the nature of 'Socialist Realism', which he deplored, with Lukacs in the 1920s/30s, a polemic which divided Marxist aesthetics into the 1960's and beyond. Therefore this analysis will address these issues: 1) what were the conditions and circumstances that moulded Brecht's creative work and aesthetics 2) the debate between Brecht and Lukacs on the nature of socialist writing 3) the content and nature of Brecht's Marxist poetry and 4) Brecht's great error of not actively supporting a worker's uprising in East Berlin in 1953 which was crushed by Russian military power and his subsequent withdrawal from the field of Marxist poetry and aesthetics and 6) Brecht's impact on the Situationist International.

Brecht was born in 1898 and would therefore experience all the major events which shaped the

20th century until 1956. Of course the first crisis was the First World War which Lenin had correctly analysed as the result of competing Capitals exporting 'finance capital' in an attempt to stabilize and expand their own capitalist economies and the inevitable conflict which would ensue i.e. World War 1. Brecht was a military orderly towards the end of the war and this experience of imperialist war and its bloody results were an important developmental factor for the young Brecht. No longer would the tradition of Goethe and Romanticism dominate German literature; the world had been objectively changed. An early poem by Brecht captures his horror of and the hypocrisy of the war (Brecht had not had access to Marxist of Leninist writing at this time) called:

'The Legend of the Dead soldier' 'And when the war was four springs old And of peace there was not a breath The soldier took the logical step And died a hero's death.

The war however was not yet done So the Kaiser was displeased to be sure That the soldier had given up like that To him it seemed premature.

The soldier is then dug up and pronounced fit for active service. Accompanied by an army Chaplin and draped in a German flag he is escorted through cheering crowds on his way back to the front line. So many were dancing around him now That the soldier could hardly be seen You could only see him from the sky above And there only stars can gleam

...

The stars are not forever there. Daylight gives new breath.' - Bertolt Brecht.

The next significant stage was Brecht being introduced, by two women who were both committed communists and also lovers of Brecht named Helene Weigel and Elisabeth Huaptmann, too classical Marxist texts. Huaptmann noted in her workbook on 25th October 1926:

'Brecht obtains works on socialism and Marxism and asks for lists of the basic works to study first.' - Elisabeth Huaptmann.

By 1929 and the Wall Street Crash which was followed by the Great Depression of the 1930's Brecht had studied Marxist economics and philosophy, some Lenin and early Mao Tse-Tung on dialectics and the role of the artist in the revolutionary struggle. But fascism was on the rise throughout Europe; now Brecht was ideologically prepared for it and in this poem delineates what he believed should be the attitude of the poet towards it:

'Within me here is a conflict between delight in the blooming apple-tree And the horror of the painter's* speeches. But only the second Drives me to my desk.' - Bertolt Brecht

*Brecht always referred to Hitler as 'the painter' because he had been a house painter.

Therefore it is possible to discern four elements in the formation of Brecht's poetry: 1) imperialist war, 2) embracing Marxism as a world-view, 3) the inevitable decline of capitalism and 4) the rise of fascism. His aesthetic was rooted in the class-struggle; you can perceive his use of everyday language and form. Brecht's position became:

'For art to become "unpolitical" means only to ally itself with the 'ruling group" - Bertolt Brecht.

However during this period there was a debate within Marxism regarding the correct 'line' on literature. Lukacs argued, in the 1920/30's, that 19th century realist novels reveal the true horrors of capitalism with 'typical' characters, hence the need for 'socialist realist' novels. Brecht disagreed and argued that the 19th century realist form is outdated and has no capacity to radicalize the oppressed and that new 'dialectical' forms were necessary. He argued in the 1930's against those who pursued the official Moscow 'line' of socialist realism:

'They are, to put it bluntly, enemies of production*. Production makes them feel uncomfortable. You never know where you are with production; production is unforeseeable. you never know what's going to come out. And they themselves don't want to produce. They want to play the apparatchik *and exercise control over other people.' - Bertolt Brecht

* For Brecht all 'production' is artistic 'production', a free 'collective act' (Brecht) * Apparatchik:Communist Party functionary in the former Soviet Union. Marx and Engels were against 'applied tendency' in literature and Marx described it as: 'The most wretched offal of socialist literature.' - Karl Marx.

Brecht used everyday language in his poetry but he poses a dialectical question, it demands a response. In the poem: 'The Sixteen-Year Old Seamstress Emma Ries before the Magistrate' Brecht exhibits two essential aspects of his poetry; 1) that it is worker centred and 2) that it incorporates a knowledge and application of Dialectical Materialism, the science of the proletariat. The poem is about a sixteen year old working class woman who has been caught distributing revolutionary leaflets. She is in a material situation, not in the vacuous spheres of bourgeois speculation. It is also the inevitable dialectical situation workers are objectively drawn into...she is in conflict with the oppressors. So here is the dialectical contradiction and how Brecht does resolve this contradiction, of course in the same manner the working class must ultimately resolve it, by revolutionary synthesis:

'As reply, she stood up and sang the Internationale When the magistrate shook his head She shouted: 'Stand up! This is the Internationale!' - Bertolt Brecht.

Therefore it is clear that in his poetry Brecht is creating a new tradition in German poetry, moving away from the themes and methods of Goethe and the Romantics and towards the future of communism.

However once ensconced in the German Democratic Republic in the role of Staatsdicher (state poet), a role he was never comfortable in Brecht made the biggest mistake of his life. It was 1953 and a spontaneous workers uprising erupted in East Berlin, after hesitation he finally supported the Stalinist elite in calling for Russian tanks to crush the revolt. He never recovered from this error and retreated into rustic silence and a poetic wasteland. But Brecht was not entirely curbed by this error and in the aftermath of the rebellion wrote one of his best anti-Stalinist/anti-capitalist poems:

'The Solution.' ...Would it not be easier In that case for the government To dissolve the people And elect another.' - Bertolt Brecht.

Finally I would like to examine the relationship between Brecht and the Situationist International's concept of detournement 'anything can be used' (Guy Debord) to disrupt the alienation within the 'Society of the Spectacle.' To put it more abruptly: 'Plagiarism is necessary. Progress implies it.' (Debord). It is necessary to place this in the context that for the Situationists art was concluded when the Spartacus League failed to bring German dada to fruition in the workers revolution of 1919. They reflected with pleasure that Brecht had commented:

'That he had made some cuts in the classics of theatre in order to make the performances more educative...closer to the revolutionary orientation we are calling for.' - Debord/Wolman.

Brecht encapsulates his aesthetic in the poem:

'Hymn to Communism'. 'It is so simple which is so difficult.' - Bertolt Brecht

On dialectics and Marxism: a philosophy for today.

'Dialectical materialism is more than a philosophical system it is a philosophy of action.'

- George Plekhanov.

Here is an explanation of the philosophical concepts which inspired and re-enforced much of the confrontation which occurred between rightist members of staff and myself. The theoreticians of the bourgeoisie, in their many manifestations from the academic to that of the padre who condones imperialism, exhibit a single and constant intellectual position in their opposition to the philosophical system of the oppressed which is dialectical materialism. The bourgeoisie are compelled to do so by their objective position in the class system of 'late-capitalism'. They are obliged not only to accumulate Capital but must, therefore, also reproduce the system of ideas. This is because ideas are created by the reproduction of the economic or material life of capitalism. In the same way the proletariat are placed in opposition to capitalism and its dominant ideas because they are economically exploited and also oppressed by bourgeois ideology. The masses are therefore drawn into opposition against capitalism and, ultimately, they are the agents of its overthrow:

'The emancipation of the proletariat is the task of the proletariat.'
- Karl Marx.

Hence the philosophy of the working class can only be forged in the furnace of the class struggle and its theoreticians must move with the motion of historical necessity which is the inevitability of proletarian revolution. So we can see how Marxist philosophy did not materialize in the minds of Marx, Engels, Plekhanov, Lenin and Trotsky spontaneously, but rather it was the consequence of the proletariat and its intellectuals learning the lessons of the class struggle.

Leon Trotsky (1879-1940), one of a vanguard of Marxist thinkers, maintained that in the process of the development of human ideas:

'Two systems of logic are worthy of attention;

the logic of Aristotle (formal logic) and the logic of Hegel (dialectical logic).
- Leon Trotsky.

More than 2,000 years ago Greek philosophers who were exploring the human mind and the natural world discovered the dialectic:

'The ancient Greeks were all natural-born dialecticians and had already analyses the most essential forms of dialectical thought'.
- Fredrick Engels.

This is clearly illustrated in the work of Heraclitus (540-480BC) who argued that:

'Everything is and is not, for everything

is fluid, is constantly changing, constantly coming into being and passing away'.
- Heraclitus..

We can locate the essence of dialectics, which is impermanence, here in the thought of Heraclitus.

The concept of 'logic' which is derived from the Greek 'logos' meaning 'word' or 'reason' formed the basis on which Aristotle (384-322 BC) constructed the model of formal logic. This became the dominant form for much human intellectual endeavour. He discerned three main laws in formal logic:

1) The Law of identity: A=A.

2) The Law of contradiction: A cannot be A and non-A.

3) The Law of the excluded middle: A is either A or non-A.

Aristotle

These three principles of logic are the foundation of modern science and mathematics. Aristotle's model of logic dominated Western thought intermittently for about 2, 000 years and appears to be 'common sense'. But 'common sense' does not look below the surface appearance of nature and the processes of History. We can begin to perceive the limitations of formal logic and to become aware of the scope of dialectical logic. As Trotsky commented:

'Dialectical understanding is not limited to the problems of daily life, but attempts to arrive at an understanding of a more complicated and drawn-our process. Dialectical and formal logic bear a relationship similar to that between higher and lower mathematics'.

- Leon Trotsky..

The limitations of formal logic or what Trotsky sometimes called 'vulgar thought' became clear with the rise of modern science. An enormous blow to the bourgeoisie and their lackeys was Charles Darwin's theory of evolution. This theory proved that one species can be transformed into another and that therefore qualitative change outside the static categories of formal logic takes place. Trotsky commented:

The fundamental flaw in vulgar thought lies in the fact that it wishes to content itself with motionless imprints of reality which consists of eternal motion.'

- Leon Trotsky..

Therefore modern science needed a philosophical system to create a theoretical model to explain its discoveries, this theory is dialectical materialism.

The roots of modern dialectics lie in radical German philosophy which had been inspired by the French revolution of 1789 and the collapse of the old order. The major thinker of this progressive wave was George F. Hegel G (1770-1831). He studied the Greek dialecticians and combined their insight about the transitory and interconnected nature of reality with German naturphilosophie or 'Philosophy of Nature'. His orientation was essentially one of metaphysics i.e. he saw reality as 'ideas' or 'spirit' rather than 'matter in motion'. However Hegel's philosophy of dialectics challenged the mechanistic ideas about motion which had become dominant. For Hegel there were three stages in the dialectical process:

1) Simple unity, the object before any change.

2) The negation, this is when the object creates its opposite.

3) The negation of the negation when the opposites are reconciled in a higher synthesis.

.

Hegel believed everything existed in the mind of God. His whole system was to show how these three moments of the dialectic, described above, are acted out by the 'Absolute Spirit' or 'Absolute Idea', which are ultimately terms for God, in History. The three stages described above became:

1) The simple unity of God.

2) God creating his negation which is Nature.

3) The unification of God and Nature through the development of human

consciousness into a higher union.

To understand this it is necessary to see it in the context of Hegel's ideas about the progress of human consciousness:

1) The simple unity of the isolated human mind.

2) The separation of the human mind from nature which Hegel called alienation.

3) Unification of the human mind with nature in the higher synthesis with the

'Absolute Spirit' or God.

Interestingly Hegel believed that this higher synthesis of the human mind, Nature and the 'Absolute Spirit' was made possible by his philosophical system. So, we can see how Hegel, as a result of the rise of radical German philosophy which was influenced by revolutionary France, created a system of ideas which transcended the limitations of formal logic and 'vulgar thought', but:

> 'Hegel fell into the illusion of conceiving the real as the product of thought, the real subject retains its autonomous existence outside the head'.
> - Karl Marx.

This means that for Marx (1818-1883) reality did not reside in thought or spirit but in the world, we see around us i.e. 'outside the head'. Hegel had advanced the concept of the dialectic; however, it was with Marx's critique of Hegel that a major leap in philosophy took place. Marx said:

> 'The dialectic is standing on its head. It must be inverted in order to discover the rational kernel within the mystical shell'.
> - Karl Marx.

It was with this analysis that Marx created the flowering of ideas which is dialectical materialism. This is the philosophy that every class-conscious worker needs in his or her daily battle with bourgeois ideology and is the system of ideas that prepares the path for worker's revolution.

Three basic laws are at the core of dialectical materialism and as a whole they form a coherent system. They comprise of:

> 'The general laws of motion and development of nature, human society and though.'
> - Fredrick Engels.

The Law of the Unity and Struggle of Opposites.
Lenin (1870-1924) summed this up:
'The condition for the knowledge
of all processes of life of the world
...in their real life is the knowledge
of them as a unity of opposites.'
- V. I. Lenin.

Let us consider two consequences of this:

a) 'non-being' must contain its opposite 'being' within itself, in the same way 'being' must contain 'non-being'. Therefore, the bourgeois argument for the necessity of a 'First Cause' to set the clockwork of the universe in motion is unnecessary because 'non-being' or 'nothing' created its opposite 'being' or 'existence' at the beginning of Time.

b) In capitalism the bourgeois and the proletariat are bound together by the system, yet they also exist as material and antagonistic opposites which creates the class struggle.

2) The Law of the Transformation of Quantity into Quality.

Engels (1820-1895) defines this law:

'We could express this by saying that
in nature...qualitative changes can only

happen with the quantitative addition or subtraction of motion'.
- Fredrick Engels.

An example of this would be that when heat is applied to water and the temperature of the water changes a quantitative change takes place, but when the water becomes steam a qualitative transformation has taken place. Similarly we can see how a series of quantitative changes takes place in a capitalist society e.g. trade union struggles and how these inevitably lead to a 'dialectical leap' or qualitative change i.e. proletarian revolution. Learning from the lessons of History Lenin developed this position:

'Capitalism creates its own gravedigger, itself creates the elements for a new system...without a 'leap' these individual elements change nothing'.
- V.I. Lenin.

Hence Lenin ascertained that there is no reformist path to socialism, there must be a 'leap', a revolution.

3) The Law of the Negation of the Negation.

In capitalism a process called the 'negation of the negation' takes place. This essentially means that the 'thesis' or first aspect of a dialectical contradiction is not destroyed by its opposite or 'antithesis' and some aspects of both the 'thesis' and the 'antitheses survive within a higher 'synthesis'. The 'negation' is in the class conflict between workers and bosses which creates the 'negation of the negation' that is proletarian revolution and socialism. The result of the 'negation of the negation' is a classless society, a society without contradictions. Marx examined the concept in Capital:

'The capitalist mode of appropriation is the first negation of individual private property based on one's labour. But capitalist production begets with the inevitability of a natural process its own negation. It is the negation of the negation.'
- Karl Marx.

What tactics should revolutionaries pursue? Ulrike Meinhoff (1934-1975) argued in 1971:

'That a pre-requisite for progress and an eventual victory of revolutionary forces is the armed struggle.'
- Ulrike Meinhoff.

But today the conditions of the class struggle have changed, and we must again win the battle of ideas, an ideological hegemony, to prepare for the inevitable revolution. Today:

'Dialectics are our sharpest weapons'.

- Fredrick Engels.

On Allen Ginsberg, 'Howl' and Trotsky.

My argument is stated succinctly and argued to its conclusion. I contest that Allen Ginsberg's Howl was, as some critics argue a popular, 'an over-simplification' of the poetry regarded by the Canon as high-quality literature. Rather, Howl formed a new genre which mirrored in its innovation other seminal moments in literature connected to changes of the 'mode of production' and had similar ramifications. The 'primitive accumulation of capital of English capitalism' that Caudwell (1937) Illusion and Reality associated with William Shakespeare, the 'bourgeois' revolutions that permeate the ideas of Wordsworth (1802) Preface to Lyrical Ballads and the shocks of Darwinism, Freud and imperialist war which informed Modernist literature, particularly the avant-garde pertinently T.S.Eliot (1922) The Waste Land. What was the problem of the writer in late-capitalism as High Modernism entered its death throes? Trotsky (1981) Art and Politics encapsulate it:

"The decline of bourgeois society means an intolerable exacerbation of social contradictions, which are transformed inevitably into personal contradictions, art suffers most from the decline and decay of bourgeois society. Art cannot save itself...But precisely in this path history has set a formidable snare for the artist."

- Trotsky (1981). p 105.

Ginsberg's reply is Howl, this is not the howl of the deranged madman outside of History, it resonates within the conversation of literature, King Lear (1603):

"Howl, howl, howl! O, you are men of stones;
Had I your tongues and eyes, I'd use them so
That heaven's vault should crack."
- Shakespeare (1603) (5.3.2.58-64).

Howl

For Carl Solomon

1

I saw the best minds of my generation destroyed by madness, starving hysterical naked, dragging themselves through the negro streets at dawn looking for an angry fix, angelheaded hipster burning for the ancient heavenly connection to the starry dynamo in the machinery of night

- Ginsberg (1956) p. 9

It is the howl of a post-WW 11 avant-garde that must inherently employ the poetic devices of literary tradition but in a different 'form'. A 'close reading' gives us several insights here. They are 'howls' of emotion, of intense emotion and resonate with William Wordsworth (1802) Preface to Lyrical Ballads:

"Poetry is the spontaneous overflow of powerful feelings: it takes its origin from emotion recollected in tranquility."

- William Wordsworth (1980) pp. 410-424.

In Shakespeare (1603) we have a reference to the howling of a man driven to madness seeking justice from 'heaven's vaults'. Ginsberg also seeks refuge in chants to the 'Holy' in Footnote to Howl. The thematic howl of a literate madness, seeking divine justice, but not locating it in a corrupted 'world' runs counterintuitive against the whole Enlightenment project. Surely Reason and empiricist science will hear the poet's words. For Americans like Ginsberg the world could not be explained in these neat confines and as a poet who had read widely, he certainly could not accept the text by text alone reductionism of the New Criticism after Hiroshima and McCarthyism, Auschwitz and Stalinism. But what differentiated Ginsberg from other 'Beat' writers in particular Kerouac was that he rejected Kerouac insistence on 'first thought, best thought'. Ginsberg was influenced by both Kerouac in terms of first impulse, but also poets like Eliot, indeed Howl' is an attempt at reproducing something of the literary magnitude of Eliot (1922) The Waste Land. I shall therefore argue against the perspective taken by advocates of Mass Culture Thesis such as the renegade ex-Trotskyist Dwight Macdonald, who argues in (1953) A Theory of Mass Culture and again (1962) Against the American Grain that the collective taste of the 'masses' was reflected in the degraded mass culture that they consumed and that, therefore, they had no 'interest' in 'High Culture'. Dwight Macdonald combined an ex-Trotskyist stance with cultural conservatism and elitism. Also, I argue against a rightist conservative position which is derived from Matthew Arnold (1869) Culture and Anarchy that has an inherent trepidation at the sound of the popular and its revolutionary proclivities. He maintained a 'secular religion' of

"The best that has been thought and said in the world."

- Arnold (1869) p 6.

Was needed to prevent the erosion of civilization. It is no accident that Arnold began his opus magnum in 1867 after a period of popular and vigorous discontent over suffrage rights. Ginsberg's reply here is the 20th century equivalent to an articulate and insurrectionary mob assailing Arnold:

"who dreamt and made incarnate gaps in Time & Space through images juxtaposed, and trapped the archangel of the soul between 2 visual images and joined the elemental verbs and set the noun and dash of consciousness together jumping with sensation of Pater Omnipotens Aeterna Deus to recreate the syntax and measure of poor human prose..."

- Ginsberg 1956 p 20.

Arnold and his Leavisities descendant would be battered and lost for words, their Weltanschauung challenged. Also, here we can perceive

Ginsberg's specialist use of 'strophes' which he defines as 'a one speech breath thought' which was akin to the jazz improvisation of Miles Davis or Charlie Parker, the black man's 'beat'. 'Form' with a regard for socio-cultural factors would be engaged by the New Historicism of Raymond Williams with his 1958 Forward to Culture and Society:

We live in an expanding culture, yet we spend much of our energy regretting the fact, rather than seeking to understand its nature and conditions.

- Lodge (1972) p. 580.

However, my position is not simply that Mass Culture Thesis and the New Criticism were erroneous, but they failed to understand the nuanced nature of 'proletarian literature' which as Trotsky illustrates is complexified:

Having broken up human relations into atoms, bourgeois society, had a great aim for itself. Personal emancipation was its name. In reality, all modern literature has been nothing but an enlargement of this theme.

- Trotsky (1981) pp. 61-62.

My position is that only the proletariat has the creative potential and socially universal nature which allowed Marx to say 'communism has solved the riddle of history' can transcend the limitations of the bourgeois intelligentsia when the social and economic conditions are ripe, that is, in a Socialist society because as Marx argued they are the 'universal class'. For the first time in history was there a social collectivity in whose interest it was to dismantle class society, because 'class' fetters on the workers of the world are their 'chains and it is in there interest 'collectively' to break those chains freeing the whole of society.

Some Marxists misunderstood the nature of the relationship between the popular and the high cultures. Adorno and Horkheimer in Dialectic of Enlightenment saw an implied analogy between Marx's concept of his fetishized 'exchange value' as a commodity and 'use-value' a 'material object'. Then they extrapolated this analogy to the relationship between popular and high culture to the detriment of the popular. Walter Benjamin is better here, seeing the potential for mechanized reproduction to free the poet from the 'aura' from his or her primitivism and allow an engaged mass readership. Also, I will draw a parallel with Maxim Gorky, Lower Depths (see Raskin 2004 p.82) and Ginsberg Howl, thus Trotsky:

"At the beginning, Gorky was imbued with the romantic individualism of the tramp. Nevertheless, he fed the early spring revolutionism of the proletariat on the eve of 1905, because he helped to awaken individuality in that class in which individuality, once awakened, seeks contact with other awakened individualities"

- Trotsky (1981) p 58-59.

For Trotsky the solution to the dichotomy of oversimplification and complexity in literature is resolved in the synthesis of revolution. Ginsberg, unlike Gorky would not be involved in a social revolution (as he may have wished) but a cultural revolution, a revolution of superstructure rather that of social base which left American capitalism weakened but intact. Louis Althusser (2006) Lenin on Philosophy and Other Essays commenting on the novels of Solzhenitsyn in (Althusser pp.153-153, 2006) makes the point of the difference between art and knowledge. Literature like Solzhenitsyn's, he argues, may have helped the reader 'feel' , 'perceive' the 'cult of personality' in the Soviet Union but doesn't provide the scientific knowledge to understand it. Althusser said art:

> In the language of Spinoza art puts the conclusions before the premises.

- Althusser (2010) p 153.

Ginsberg achieves this by employing and developing poetic devices, Walt Whitman's 'long-line' which is a non-metrical line of poetry of length which usually employs enjambment, anaphora which is a 'figure of repetition' in which the same word is repeated as in Part 1 'Who' usually at the beginning successive 'lines, clauses or sentences' , cauda or the tail-rhyme stanza and a surrealist juxtaposition of images such as 'helium jukebox' (1956).Also Ginsberg aspired to create: 'Certain combinations of words and rhythms actually have:

> an electrochemical reaction on the body, which could catalyze specific states of consciousness.

- Ginsberg (2001) p.31.

Brain Jackson (2010) argues: 'the most compelling example of reading "Howl" -specially out loud – is the sene of time shifting from the prosaic to the mythical. Lines such as:

who walked all night with their shoes full of blood on the snow deck docks waiting for a door in the East River to open to a room full of steamheat opium,

- Ginsberg (1956) p. 15

He continues:

the rhythmic and trouping artifice of Howl constitute...a suspension of time in which the natural laws occur'.

- Jackson (2010) pp 312-313).

Therefore, I maintain that Ginsberg poetry contradicted the ideas of thinkers such as Mathew Arnold, T. S. Eliot, and William Empson's Seven Types of Ambiguity on the Right and renegade Trotskyists like Dwight MacDonald and neo-Marxists Adorno and Horkheimer. I suggest that the neo-Marxism of Louis Althusser enhanced my general understanding of the positioning of the debates regarding the poetry of Ginsberg, particularly Howl and that in this context it is possible to comprehend him in a lineage of literati,

Finally I argue that Ginsberg created not a simplified poetry for mass consumption and 'narcotization' of literary consciousness, but formed the matrix for a new genre of second wave of 20th century avant-garde writers who took and added to the High Modernism of 1910-39 and created a wedge into the monotonous conformity of 1950's poetry. Even poets like Sylvia Plath and Anne Sexton who were writing confessional verse which was challenging some conventions in terms of gender and 'content' i.e. mental illness Plath ([1963] 2004) Ariel and Sexton's (1960) 'To Bedlam and part way back' were not really contesting the terrain of bourgeois hegemony. Ginsberg did shift the aesthetics of the hegemonic superstructure cultural construct in favour of the 'progressive', he unlocks much in this poem, but he was unable to create a social revolution. I conclude that the task can only be brought to fruition by the self-emancipation of the proletariat as Leon Trotsky argues in Literature and Revolution:

"Under Socialism, Literature and art will be tuned to a different key such as disinterested friendship, this will be the mighty ringing chords of Socialist poetry. However, does not an excess of solidarity, as the Nietzscheans fear, threaten to degenerate man into a sentimental, passive, herd animal? No, not at all. The powerful force of competition this, in bourgeois society, has the character of market competition, will not disappear in a Socialist society, but, to use the language of psycho-analysis, will be sublimated, Art then will become the most perfect ethos for progressive life-building of life in every field."

- Leon Trotsky (1981). p 60.

The Beats could not vanquish 'Moloch' (essentially, 'Capitalism') but they did undermine, disrupted what Lyotard calls it 'meta-narrative' creating the conditions for minority narratives. Nevertheless, only socialist transformation as understood in the aesthetic writings of Trotsky can create authentic liberation for all of humanity. We may read Ginsberg as a disappointed, reincarnated Maxim Gorky lapsing into a hope for Nirvana with a juxtaposition of the social and questioning 'Who' of Part 1, with the devastation of Moloch only relieved with the introspection of fifteen iambs in two sentences, one 'long-line' without punctuation except the repeated and insistent exclamation marks after each Holy! Footnote to Howl pp 27-8. Ginsberg did provide hope in a new 'beatification' of language within Historical Materialism's philosophy, a new Communist International to resurrect Trotsky's Fourth International...

'holy the Fifth International!' (ibid).

Bibliography.

Adorno, T and Horkheimer, M. ([1944] 1979) Dialectic of Enlightenment, trans. by Cumming, London: New Left Books.

Althusser, L (2006) Lenin and Philosophy and other essays, Dahl: Aakar Books.

Arnold, M ([1869] 1993) Culture and Anarchy and Other Writings, ed. by S.Collini, Cambridge: Cambridge University Press.

Caudwell, C ([1937]1977) Illusion and Reality, London: Lawrence & Wishart.

Eliot, T.S. ([1920] 1960) The Sacred Wood, London: Macmillan.

Empson, W ([1936] 1966) Seven types of Ambiguity, New York: New Directions.

Ginsberg, A ([1956] 2002) Howl and Other Poems, San Francisco: City Lights.

Ginsberg, A (2001) Spontaneous Mind: Selected Interviews 1958-1996. New York: HarperCollins.

Jackson, A, Modernist Looking: Surreal Impressions in the Poetry of Allen Ginsberg Texas Studies in Literature and Language, Vol. 52, No. 3, Fall 2010.

Lodge, J (1972) 20th Century Literary Criticism: A Reader, London: Longman.

Lyotard, J.F. (1984) The Postmodern Condition: A Report on Knowledge, trans, by G. Bennington and B. Massumi, Manchester, Manchester University Press.

MacDonald, D (1953) A Theory of Mass Culture, Rosenberg, R. and White D.W (1957) (eds), Mass Culture: The popular arts in America, New York: MacMillan.

MacDonald, D (1962) Against the American Grain, New York: A Da Capo Paperback.

Plath, S (2004) Ariel: The Restored Edition, London: Faber and Faber.

Ruskin, J (2004) American Scream: Allen Ginsberg's Howl and the making of the Beat Generation, Berkley, University of California Press.

Sexton, A (1960) To Bedlam and part way back, Boston: Houghton Mifflin Company.

Shakespeare, W (1603) King Lear. Pugh, T and Johnston, Margret R. (2014) Literary Studies A Practical Guide, New York: Routledge.

Trotsky, L (1981) On Literature and Art, New York Pathfinder Press.

Wordsworth W (1980) Selected Poetry and Prose of William Wordsworth, New York: Meriden Books.

"This thing of darkness I acknowledge mine" : Jungian analysis of The Tempest (Prospero and Caliban).

"Tumult and peace, the darkness and light - Were all the workings of one mind"

- Wordsworth.

This analysis will argue that Shakespeare's "The Tempest" functions on many levels:

1) the tempest as an allegory 2) that the play can be understood, persuasively, by applying a model of Jungian psychology to it 3) in this context Caliban is a projection of Prospero's unconscious and, finally 4) that Prospero's achieves "individualization" by accepting his "darkness"."(by individualization I mean) becoming a single homogenous being...Becoming one's own sel...Coming into selfhood"- Jung). .

Firstly, the backdrop to the drama is conflict: a storm rages. The idea of a tempest is embedded in the Western cultural tradition which emanates, to an extent, from the Judeo- Christian perspective of which Shakespeare would have been aware. This is manifest in the Old Testament where a storm is perceived as the consequence of repression of natural forces or a birth trauma:

or who shut up the sea with doors, when
it brake forth, as if it had issued out of the womb.
                    - The Bible.

However, Shakespeare enhances the traditional image to give it an egalitarian orientation:

"What cares these roarers for the name of King?"

- Shakespeare.

This storm is a symptom of inner conflict within Prospero and is therefore, in turn, his allegorical reality.

The Tempest) is an example of allegory the leading characters are not merely typical but symbolic.

- Lowell.

The world of symbols is significant in psychology; Freud believed that they existed in the "unconscious" and were repressed material expelled from the "ego". However, Jung developed this concept to embrace a "collective unconscious"; a world of primal images which occur consistently in humanity's mythology and religions. These recurring or primal symbols he called "archetypes." The philosophical dimension of Jung's psychology can be located in Plato's „Theory of Forms" ,here the "Idea" exists in a pure "Form" beyond the material world in the same way that Jung's symbols exist beyond consciousness. But Jung expanded his theory of symbols to describe a more precise element of the unconscious:

"a symbol was a particular manifestation of something unknown".

- McLynn.

One of these "particular" symbols, for this analysis, is the island where the drama is enacted which is a "projection" (Jung) of inner worlds:

.... the isle is full of noises
… Sometimes a thousand twanging instruments
   Will hang about my ears.
                                    - Shakespeare.

The onomatopoeia of "twanging" enforces this sense.

On the island the relationship between Prospero and Caliban was an exploitative one. Prospero treats Caliban as a slave by day and torments him at night. I would like to examine their relationship in the context of contemporary cultural sources. Firstly, Caliban is an anagram of "cannibal", spelt "canibal" in Shakespeare's era, secondly that Shakespeare would have been aware of, in particular, Montaigne's essay: „Of the Cannibals" in which "primitive" societies are seen as natural until tainted by civilization:

" Montaigne is saying that the life of the South American Indians proves that mankind is capable of living peacefully, happily and humanly without the constraint of law, or the institution of private property".

                                    - Middleton Murry.

This is reflected by Gonzalo"s speech on utopia:

> I'll the commonwealth... I would admit; no name of magistrate ...
>
> ... Riches, poverty, service none. No occupation, all men idle.

Shakespeare.

Hence Caliban can be perceived as a member of a, potentially, utopian community and Prospero as the corrupting force of civilization. Thus, Caliban is perceived as the "primitive" (unconscious) and Prospero as civilization (conscious). This idea can be developed by applying Jung's conception of the feminine perspective which he believed to emanate from the "Great Mother" archetype:

She has always been connected with the moon and the earth...

she was and is the matrix from which all is born.

> - Von der Heydt.

This analysis maintains that, following Jung, the feminine is the source of creativity {See Robert Graves (1961) for a theory of the feminine as Lunar Muse"}. Therefore it is possible to argue that Caliban is in tune with his, to use Jung's term, Anima (the unconscious feminine) i.e. the creative/primitive (Earth) aspect of his psyche:

" . .Caliban! Thou (being of the) Earth speak ...

> - Shakespeare.

Caliban can therefore be comprehended as the source of the play's creativity. This is stressed, by Shakespeare, as Caliban speaks in poetry and Prospero in prose. Caliban's role as a vehicle for creative energy and of his being, therefore, in tune with nature and poetry is illustrated in the following passage:

....in dreaming, methought the clouds would open ...
Ready to drop on me; when I wak"d, I cried to dream again.

- Shakespeare.

This passage is beautiful in its poetic innocence. Coleridge elaborated on this aspect of Caliban's being:

Caliban...is a sort of creature of the earth...He is a man in the sense of imagination.

- Coleridge.

However, Prospero's attitude towards Caliban could have been influenced by the attempted rape, by Caliban, of his daughter Miranda.

In mine own cell till thou dast seek to violate the honour of my child.

Shakespeare.

But some Jungian theorists have maintained that this was itself a projection by Prospero of incestuous feelings onto Caliban:

"Incest; the molestation and rape of one's daughter. Miranda had reached womanhood with herself and her father as the only two humans in their world".

— Beck.

Why then is Caliban defined as "other" or "dark". in the play? The Jungian concept of "The Shadow" provides an explanation. Jung explains his concept:

The shadow personifies everything the subject refuses to acknowledge about himself.
— Jung.

The ideas that are not accepted become repressed into an unconscious complex: the shadow. There are, essentially, two methods which Jung thought people employ to address their "Shadow": 1) projection i.e. projecting your "shadow "onto another person. or 2) "integration", i.e. the accepting your "shadow" as part of the "Self." Jung thought the latter lead to selfhood and "individualization". Prospero has repressed his "shadow", his moon and Earth dimensions, the Anima which is the source of creativity. The consequences of this were 1) becoming introspective and interested in using manipulation (magic):

And to my state grew stranger, being transported
And rapt in secret studies.
— Shakespeare

2) projecting his "shadow" onto Caliban and using abusive language to describe him: "Thou most lying slave...

Filth thou art

- Shakespeare.

This is the generalized "tempest".

Caliban can be seen as a projection of Prospero's "shadow", his unconscious complex which is both creative and destructive.

Prospero is afraid of Caliban. He is afraid because he knows that his encounter with Caliban is largely his encounter with himself.

- Singh.

Prospero has a choice: either his unconscious will overwhelm him and he will descend into madness or he can integrate his "shadow", Caliban, into himself. Prospero chooses the path of self-integration:

This thing of darkness I acknowledge mine.

Shakespeare.

An encounter between Virginia Woolf and some Poets.

> Communism in the truer sense is an effort to think, and think into action, human society as an organism (not a machine which is too static a metaphor).
> - Louis MacNeice

I shall argue that a dialectical tension existed between Woolf's understanding of the aesthetic nature of poetry which as she articulated it in *The Leaning Tower* (1940) was essentially a *Victorian poetic* which I argue is flawed as it was an Aestheticist view and was contradicted by the complexified literary method presented by many writers of W. H. Auden's generation as illustrated in Christopher Caudwell *Illusion and Reality* (1937), which I favour, and Auden *Introduction to The Oxford Book of Light Verse* (1938) who developed to a greater and lesser degree respectively a dialectical materialist view of British poetry. I shall show that in Skelton's anthology *Poetry of The Thirties* (2000) Auden *Spain* (c. 1937) wrote a complexified poetics consistent with this literary methodology. However, this cannot as Woolf argues be separated from the work of T.S. Eliot. Indeed, it is contextualized by the Modernist poetry of Eliot (1919) *Prufrock and Other Observations* and also in his masterpiece The Wasteland in 1922. I also maintain that because of the material contradictions of Modernity and the 'reflection' of this in literature created in the iconic writer of modernist poetry, T.S. Eliot, a contradictory consciousness in his literary output. This can be perceived in the tensions between his revolutionary stylistic innovations and his 'conservative' literary criticism even before his shift to Anglo-Catholicism. These can be comprehended in the context of contradictory and contending Modernisms reflected by the material contradictions into the ideological 'superstructure'. This contestation between the old and new productive forces in a period of social transformation can be manifested as fragmentation of the consciousness which can be seen in Eliot which mirrored the crisis of post WW1 European capitalism. The revolutionary and the reactionary forces which emanated from the material conditions contented for hegemonic cultural dominance.

The methodology I employ in this analysis was encapsulated initially by Marx in the Preface to *A Contribution to the Critique of Political Economy* (1859):

In the social production of their life, men enter into definite relations that are indispensable and independent of their will, relations of production which correspond to a definite stage of development of their material forces... The mode of production conditions the social, political and intellectual life process in general.

- Marx

The creation of a new mode of production which developed into finance capitalism unleashing yet more competing social and economic classes but also contending models of literary production. This upheaval was characterized in Lenin (1916) *Imperialism, The Highest Stage of Capitalism* as 'moribund capitalism'. It is the crisis of modern in which he also described as 'late capitalism'. Ernst Fischer in *The Necessity of Art: a Marxist Approach* (1978) applies this pertinently to art:

In a decaying society, art, if it is to be truthful, must also reflect decay. And unless it wants to break faith with its social function, art must show the world as changeable.

- Fischer

The European 'Mind' was not the homogenised entity claimed by Eliot in *Tradition and Individual Talent* (1919) with its individual traditions, it was a system torn by war and crisis:

The whole of the literature of Europe from Homer and within it the
whole of the literature of his own country has a simultaneous order. This historical sense which is timeless as well as temporal.

- T.S. Eliot

The revolutionary nature of *Prufrock and Other Observations* (1917) which in there form and content challenged the hegemony of the bourgeoisie which he was paradoxically defending in his conservative criticism. T.S. Eliot was the personification of the contradiction of literature in 'late-capitalism': both avant-garde yet reactionary. The writers of the 1930's where caught between these opposing forces. However many did not sit on or lean against an ivory tower as Woolf had argued, but volunteered with the International Brigades or the more independent P.O.U.M. to fight Fascism in the Spanish Civil War as Orwell in *Homage to Catalonia* (1938) illustrates vividly. Some of the writers Woolf critiques in *The Leaning Tower* (1940) did as she points out:

They feel compelled to preach, if not by their living, at least by their writing, the creation of a society in which everyone is equal and everyone is free. It explains the pedagogic, the didactic, the loud-speaker strain of their poetry.

- Woolf.

Auden had articulated in these words the milieu which many of these writers inhabited included a belief that it was necessary to transform the 'means of production' in order to solve the malady of the estrangement of literary production, in particular that of the poet:

In such a society it, and, in such alone, will it be possible for the poet, without sacrificing any of the subtleties or his integrity, to write poetry which is simple, clear and gay. For poetry which is at the same time light and adult can only be written in a society which is both integrated and free

- Auden.

Eliot had maintained in *The Perfect Critic* (1920) that:

The creative writer and citric should frequently be the for same person.

- T.S. Eliot.

Here Eliot is undermining the very position he articulated as the theory of the 'depersonalized poet', the poet cannot, I would maintain, be both an anonymous 'poet persona' and then self-consciously create a body of criticism about this work. These inconsistencies in Eliot are at the heart of his project for creating a *modern classicist poetics.* The conflicts, contestation and ambiguities are thus evident in Woolf's essay *The Leaning Tower* for three reasons, firstly Woolf's understanding of Romanticism is flawed in that she does not comprehend the revolutionary nature of *Preface* to Lyrical Ballads written by Wordsworth in 1802 which rather than positing the solitary aesthete of Woolf's essay he wrote:

The principal object, then, which I proposed to myself in these poems were to choose incidents and situations from common life, and to relate or describe them, throughout, as far as was possible, in a selection of language really used by men.
- Wordsworth.

In its context at a time of revolutionary tumult by contesting Classicism as the dominant verse form is was radical as opposed to conservative. Secondly when she wrote *The Leaning Tower* the USSR were not supporting Britain at the beginning of WW11, they only did so later in 1941. In that context I would argue some of the comments about Leftist poet 'winning' and 'bleating' against the system that educated them is unbecoming of a great woman of letters and finally she does not anticipate David Hume's philosophical critique of her version of the why do you stay argument, 'a society which would like to kick them off its back' Virginia Woolf where Hume likened dissenters to captives on a ship who were unable to get off (Hume 1748). In opposition to Auden who in *Memory of W .B. Yeats* (1939) wrote 'poetry makes nothing happen'. I would argue following Bertolt Brecht:

Art is not a mirror to reflect reality,

Rather it is a hammer to shape it.

> Brecht.

I shall use a 'close reading' of Auden, Spain to make my argument. I agree with Christopher Caudwell in his exposition of the essential feature regarding the social nature of Art:

Art has social functions. This is not a Marxist demand but arises from the very way art forms are defined. Only those things that are recognized as art forms which have a conscious social function.

> Caudwell.

My 'close-reading' which illustrates my thesis is Auden, *Spain* (c. 1937), I adhere to Caudwell's insight regarding the general writing of poetry, Auden and the Audenesque in in the 1930's when he wrote:

> But a prerequisite is to attain a world-view that will become general... This Auden, Spender and Lewis have so far failed to do.
>
> - Caudwell.

That is they didn't embrace and understand the methodology of dialectical materialism and hence their later Rightward turn. Auden *Spain* (c, 1937) of which he Auden would in 1965 refer to this poem 'as a bad influence' thus retrospectively editing his work, at least in ideological term. But Auden is not here writing a simplistic didactic poem. The 'force' of his 'foregrounding' of the signifiers 'yesterday', 'today' and 'tomorrow' for the 'signified' 'History'. He uses these refrains in a particular synaptic pattern throughout the poem to create a sense both the immediacy of the Spanish Civil War and the larger overarching context of human history. He juxtaposes the old 'Yesterday' in which Medieval and Romantic are represented by two troupes as follows and contrasted with the urgency of Spain during the Spanish Civil War and revolution:

Yesterday the prayer at sunset
And the adoration of the madman.
But today the struggle.
 - Auden.

We can also see his use of assonance to stress both the contrast but also paradoxically the continuity of paradigmatic model: with the 'ya' of 'Yesterday' and ay of 'prayer' and the 'ae' of 'Sunset'.

The controversial nature of phrases like:

...the young poets exploding like bombs.

- Auden.

Is to an extent overemphasised as it is a simile used as a poetic device and therefore means 'exploding with ideas' as well as an encouragement to join the International Brigades and:

The conscious acceptance of guilt in the necessary murder.

- Auden.

Here Auden is writing as much the Freudian psychoanalytical poet as the recruiting sergeant. So here he makes 'conscious' the 'necessary' Oedipus or Elektra Complex as a poetic Bildungsroman or 'coming of age'. Orwell is missing the point in regard of poetry here, I would suggest:

so much of this sort of left-wing thought of playing with fire by people who don't even know the fire is hot.

- George Orwell.

It is apparent from this couplet which forms the end of a quatrain and his use of alliteration and metaphor. The 'o's reinforce the agency and 'world-historic mission' to coin Fredrick Engels phrase of the proletariat with the poetic mode of the post-revolutionary 'refreshing river.' However, the enjambment: the/Organizer is a little dissonant and suggests a wariness of the 'Party organizer.' We can understand Auden's poem not as a crude piece of didactic writing, but a complicated and well-constructed piece of verse. Obviously, he was in favour of the International Brigades, but this is poetry not sloganizing. Indeed, it is only by with the proletariat acting as the agent of social transformation that we have a 'new' poetry:

> The social revolution... cannot draw poetry from the past, only the future.
>
> - Marx.

www.ingramcontent.com/pod-product-compliance
Lightning Source LLC
Chambersburg PA
CBHW020653220526
45464CB00001B/415